C0-AUQ-748

LAW AND POLITICS IN THE INTERNATIONAL SOCIETY

Volume 32, Sage Library of Social Research

SAGE LIBRARY OF SOCIAL RESEARCH

1. **DAVID CAPLOVITZ:** The Merchants of Harlem
2. **JAMES N. ROSENAU:** International Studies and the Social Sciences
3. **DOUGLAS E. ASHFORD:** Ideology and Participation
4. **PATRICK J. McGOWAN and HOWARD B. SHAPIRO:** The Comparative Study of Foreign Policy
5. **GEORGE A. MALE:** The Struggle for Power
6. **RAYMOND TANTER:** Modelling and Managing International Conflicts
7. **ANTHONY JAMES CATANESE:** Planners and Local Politics
8. **JAMES RUSSELL PRESCOTT:** Economic Aspects of Public Housing
9. **F. PARKINSON:** Latin America, the Cold War, and the World Powers, 1945-1973
10. **ROBERT G. SMITH:** Ad Hoc Governments
11. **RONALD GALLIMORE, JOAN WHITEHORN BOGGS, and CATHIE JORDAN:** Culture, Behavior and Education
12. **HOWARD W. HALLMAN:** Neighborhood Government in a Metropolitan Setting
13. **RICHARD J. GELLES:** The Violent Home
14. **JERRY L. WEAVER:** Conflict and Control in Health Care Administration
15. **GEBHARD LUDWIG SCHWEIGLER:** National Consciousness in Divided Germany
16. **JAMES T. CAREY:** Sociology and Public Affairs
17. **EDWARD W. LEHMAN:** Coordinating Health Care
18. **CHARLES G. BELL and CHARLES M. PRICE:** The First Term
19. **CLAYTON P. ALDERFER and L. DAVE BROWN:** Learning from Changing
20. **L. EDWARD WELLS and GERALD MARWELL:** Self-Esteem
21. **ROBERT S. ROBINS:** Political Institutionalization and the Integration of Elites
22. **WILLIAM R. SCHONFELD:** Obedience and Revolt
23. **WILLIAM C. McCREADY and ANDREW M. GREELEY:** The Ultimate Values of the American Population
24. **F. IVAN NYE:** Role Structure and Analysis of the Family
25. **PAUL WEHR and MICHAEL WASHBURN:** Peace and World Order Systems
26. **PATRICIA R. STEWART:** Children in Distress
27. **JUERGEN DEDRING:** Recent Advances in Peace and Conflict Research
28. **MOSHE M. CZUDNOWSKI:** Comparing Political Behavior
29. **JACK D. DOUGLAS:** Investigative Social Research
30. **MICHAEL STOHL:** War and Domestic Political Violence
31. **NANCY E. WILLIAMSON:** Sons or Daughters
32. **WERNER LEVI:** Law and Politics in the International Society
33. **DAVID L. ALTHEIDE:** Creating Reality
34. **ALLAN LERNER:** The Politics of Decision-Making
35. **PHILIP E. CONVERSE:** The Dynamics of Party Support
36. **CHARLES L. NEWMAN and BARBARA R. PRICE:** Jails and Drug Treatment
37. **CLARENCE L. ABERCROMBIE III:** The Military Chaplain
38. **MARK GOTTDIENER:** Planned Sprawl
39. **ROBERT L. LINEBERRY:** Equality and Urban Policy

Law and Politics in the International Society

WERNER LEVI

Volume 32
SAGE LIBRARY OF
SOCIAL RESEARCH

For information address:

SAGE PUBLICATIONS, INC.
275 South Beverly Drive
Beverly Hills, California 90212

SAGE PUBLICATIONS LTD
St George's House / 44 Hatton Garden
London EC1N 8ER

Printed in the United States of America

Library of Congress Cataloging in Publication Data

Levi, Werner, 1912-
Law and politics in the international society.

(Sage library of social research ; v. 32)
Includes bibliography, p. 173
1. International law. 2. International relations.
I. Title.
JX3140.L48 341 76-22580
ISBN 0-8039-0617-X
ISBN 0-8039-0618-8 pbk.

FIRST PRINTING

TABLE OF CONTENTS

INTRODUCTION

Traditionally, international lawyers have treated their subject in sovereign independence from others. Students of international politics have tended to relegate international law into the back pages of their books. In this book, an attempt is made to treat international law as an integral part of international politics, in the hope of helping in the understanding of both. Such an attempt is not new. Charles de Visscher, Percy Corbett, Morton Kaplan, Nicholas deB. Katzenbach, Julius Stone, Georg Schwarzenberger, Stanley Hoffmann, Wesley Gould, Michael Barkun, and William Coplin are among the distinguished scholars who have dealt with the interaction between international law and politics. On the assumption that there is a need for further exploration of this topic, this book has been written.

Because the focus here is on the relationship between law and politics, neither receives preferred, specialized treatment. The nature of international law is interpreted as a dependent of the nature of international politics. Both are assumed to perform social functions and to be creations of men. An investigation of the social foundation of law and politics, and of the attitudes of men toward the international society, represents therefore an important part of the present enterprise.

No preconceived theory of politics or law explains the approach taken in this book. Instead, an examination of the practice of states and, to some extent, international organizations has led to the description of the nature of both politics and law in their interrelation. The reality of international law and politics is, after all, in the behavior of states. It may be logical or illogical, consequent or contradictory, and, by some subjective standard, good or bad. But it may not correspond to any particular theory or any particular moral system. Forcing it into one might falsify the picture of reality. The usefulness of such an approach should be as an indicator of why international law and international politics are what they are and, hence, what measures might be taken for their desired improvement.

W.L.

Chapter 1

THE NATURE AND FUNCTION OF LAW

The apparent wish of men and women is to survive collectively because they wish to live individually. An indispensable prerequisite for social existence is social order. Social order means regularity and predictability in the behavior of the society's members. Such behavior cannot be created by the spontaneous or rational decisions of each member. Only social action can produce it and every society has instruments for doing so. Among them is law, a set of binding rules enjoining a certain behavior on all subjects under specified and comparable conditions. The goal and major function of law is to create social order by commanding requisite behavior. Law therefore appears wherever men coexist in contact, whether this be in the neighborhood or the world. But it may not always be easy to discover the law. There are societies, mainly so-called primitive societies and, to some extent, the international society, whose institutions are quite undifferentiated. They may lack specific organs for creating, interpreting, and applying law. They never lack binding rules for social behavior, however. It may merely be difficult to discover where and exactly what the rules are.

Law--Made by Man

In all modern societies, law can be found in codes, binding custom, treaties and conventions, general principles universally valid or particular rules agreed to between the parties, and also in legal judgments and administrative rulings. But wherever law arises and can be found, it is a human product. Sometimes ultimate roots of law are claimed to be in nature or divine revelation. This belief in natural law has greatly influenced juristic theory. But as a social fact the claim is a device the more incontrovertibly to legitimate law. Law is always formulated and promulgated by men. Men always define its meaning. They are responsible for its quality and they are capable of changing it. The given social system determines which men are involved and how. Many alternatives exist as to who the maker and interpreter of law shall be. Men also have choices regarding the method for making the law, the manner in which law shall regularize behavior, and the means by which law shall be interpreted, applied, and enforced.

The legal will of men is restricted by two major limitations. One is the conditions over which men have no control, including the physical laws of nature. The other is the inherent function of law. A rule enjoining behavior contrary to the purpose of law, for instance, commanding disorderly behavior, would not be law. Revolutionary or anarchic law is the epitome of lawless behavior. Laws of war are law if they aim at making warfare regular and orderly. Making any orderly society possible requires a certain behavior so that some laws can be found in any society—for instance, that agreements must be kept or that murder is forbidden. These limitations on the law-making will of men are inherent in the nature of any society, although it may be difficult to discover what the least common denominator for social order is. But if men wish to maintain any society, these laws must prevail. (They should not be confused with natural law which allegedly defines a particular form of social order.) They are unyielding (ius cogens) and can be abolished only at the risk of destroying the society. Beyond these few indispensable rules, the formulations of laws can be as numerous as the ways in which men can organize their societies and pursue their interests.

Once men have chosen these ways, have decided upon the nature of their society, they will formulate the laws required to maintain and develop it. This close connection between a particular society and its laws makes any objective definition of a law's meaning fairly irrelevant. This must be discovered in the law's social context (thus, the identical behavior may be interpreted as stealing, borrowing, or sharing by different societies; the definition of obscene behavior is notoriously dependent upon the contemporary state of the society). For this reason, courts, including the International Court of Justice, in interpreting laws and treaties, refer to the context, to the purpose and objective, of the rules to be interpreted. If you want to be sure what a treaty means said Elihu Root (1914), and the same applies to law, "learn out of what conflicting public policies the words of the treaty had their birth; what arguments were made for one side or the other, what concessions were yielded in the making of the treaty."

This close connection also indicates that law is the creature of its society even while it regulates its creator, which means that men will the law as well as their subjection to it. But men are not omnipotent. Any one generation can produce only limited change. Social change is gradual and sluggish, but nevertheless subject to human manipulation. Each succeeding generation adds or subtracts an increment. The important point is that social institutions, including laws, must be understood as human enterprises. Law and the legal system cannot be treated as independent entities—except in a limited technical sense—apart from the human beings in whom they alone have reality. The strengths and the weaknesses of the law, the good or bad functioning of the legal system, have their causes in the people from whom they stem and whose ends they are intended to serve. When, for instance, international law is criticized as inadequate for maintaining a peaceful orderly international society, the burden is on those groups among the world's peoples whose behavior makes the society, not upon the law.

Problems in formulating laws are usually problems located in human characteristics. Their solution then would lie not in the manipulation of formulations, but in changes of attitudes, sentiments, interests, motivations, or whatever human factors produce the problems. An unstable polity, for instance, cannot be made stable by manipulating constitutions but by manipulating institutions. Or, the imperfections of the United Nations are due not to the Charter as much as to the manner in which the Charter is used. Laws become obsolete because they lose meaning in the light of social change and new behavior; or they are a dead letter before ever becoming effective when they do not correspond to human needs and interests. The efficacy of law depends much upon its adaptation to social decisions it is intended to translate into behavior.[1] When this continuous interplay is ignored, there will be a disharmony between the law and the prevailing social behavior, which can usually be adjusted by a change in the law, rarely by a change in social behavior. Such disharmony can frequently be found in the international society due to the low interests actually pursued by states, and the high principles they publicly confess and must therefore use as the basis of international law. Its most extreme case is the untrammeled pursuit of national interests even when this is irreconcilable with a stable and orderly international society. No legal system can cater to the pursuit of such contradictory interests by the members of the society.[2] The broader problem involved here is that the efficacy of a legal system depends greatly upon how well it can cope with some basic aspects of human nature; and that some of these aspects (for instance, insistent pursuit of mutually exclusive interests) potentially defy effective legal regulation and must be handled by other controls.

The first among these aspects of human nature, and of special relevance to international law, is an urge to be free from restraint upon behavior. The paradox results that freedom for any member of the society is possible only by some restraint upon all. Law is one such restraint. Often, as Nietzsche pointed out, the individual desires social order so that restraints to produce it will be part of his will and not experienced as restraints. The fact remains, however, that objectively every law eliminates a choice of behavior, and would be futile if it did not (Goodwin, 1974: 29; Hoffmann, 1971: 35). For this reason it may be resented, resisted, and disobeyed. Nevertheless, men have to choose among their goals and interests, and the means to achieve them, because the law will never grant them unrestricted behavior.

A second aspect, also important for international law, is that men have competing and different interests, holding them with varying intensities and therefore with varying willingness to compromise. Because these interests can never all be fully satisfied, politics and law arise. Politics then settles who gets what, when, and how (to use Harold Lasswell's [1963] expression), and law turns the settlement into obligatory behavior. By regulating behavior, law also determines, at least indirectly, whether and how interests may be satisfied. People with different interests will therefore disagree on the desirability of specific laws. The rich more than the poor are likely to support laws guaranteeing a free market and private property. States with large navies and merchant fleets are likely to advocate freedom of the seas and to narrow territorial limits more enthusiastically than states not so well endowed. When such differences about special interests are transferred to interests in the total character of the society they then involve the entire social, including the legal, order. They form the stuff of political conflict, with the outcome forming the substance of the legal order. Because this outcome is rarely equally advantageous to all groups in the society, the struggle for power includes the ability to make the laws as part of the attempt to control the social controls. What frequently delimits the power struggle arising from differing interests in the nature of the particular society is the interest shared by virtually all members in having a society at all. The laws preserving the society will therefore be the most effective. But a coinciding, common interest among states in maintaining an orderly, peaceful international society is very weak and the effectiveness of international law is affected thereby.

A third aspect of human nature is the inequality of men. As its consequence their condition in their society is also unequal. Some are more powerful than others and able to gain control of the legal system. They will exploit it for their own purposes and thereby provoke others to wrest that control from its possessors. An unending struggle follows, threatening the stability of the society. No legal system can solve this problem adequately. The international legal system postulates the legal equality of states. But the "less equal" weaker states often attempt to turn this legal equality into real, substantive equality, without much success. Inequalities among states are eagerly maintained and exploited by states in a superior status (Levi, 1974a: 39-45). Thus, the problem of inequality is even more acute and insoluble for international than for national law.

These basic and universal aspects of human nature, affecting all social groups, give rise to law in the first place, but also endanger the success of the law. This difficulty is aggravated for international law because a community of interest as a base for effective law is extremely limited; however, the wish of states for freedom from restraint, their diversity of interests, and their inequality are pronounced.

To wit, the desire of states for freedom of action has shaped the entire international system and dominates its institutions. The desire's objective expression is sovereignty; its subjective foundation is nationalism. States subordinate the welfare of the international society to their own. Concern for the international welfare exists normally only when it serves national purposes. When those of several states coincide, a community of interests may exist, although the interests are likely to be alike rather than common. Most often national interests are individual, endowed with a life and death quality, and mutually exclusive. Even when less than "vital" interests are at stake they permeate all international behavior whose aim is to guarantee the conditions of national primacy over international welfare. The result is a struggle for power whose minimal goal is the protection of states against unwanted influence from without and whose maximum goal is to dominate the international society. Its fierceness might be extenuated to the extent that an increasing volume of like national interests allows mutualities and reciprocities among states to replace confrontations. While the struggle lasts, the inequality among states becomes highly relevant. It enables states to engage in competition for superior power with some prospect of success. Might not only makes right (which it does everywhere), it also becomes arbitrary and flouts right. Powerful states impose their will upon weaker states. If they choose to clothe their dominance in legal form, the resulting law will be resisted. The revolt of the new states against the international law prevailing at their birth is good evidence of this situation.

In sum, the undisciplined exercise of behavioral freedom, supreme pursuit of selfish national interests only occasionally tempered by like international interests, and unhindered exploitation of inequalities are creating a society in which the effect of these socially unfavorable aspects of human nature is enhanced. The centrifugal forces of a society are strengthened (e.g., no central government). All social controls are weakened (e.g., moral principles are not applied to foreigners, or permissive different moral principles are created for states). International law is bound to reflect such social behavior. It becomes weak to the point of being ineffective at times, or else so permissive as to be no hindrance to arbitrary behavior (as when states use violence for self-defense, which is undefined for obvious reasons).

Under the conditions of the international society the weakness of law as a social control is shared by other social controls. There is no strength in any to compensate for the weakness of the others. This will become evident when an examination of morality and custom as social controls under the conditions of the international society will show how much weaker their impact is upon the international than upon any national society.

Law, Custom, and Morality

Law, custom, and morality try to fashion individual behavior into regularities and predictability to fit the prevailing patterns of social behavior. This purpose is common to them. They differ in the manner of achieving it and in the efficacy of their functioning. But these differences are not always easy to detect, especially when a society, like the international, lacks specialized institutions (educational, legislative, religious, and the like) for producing social controls. For this reason, Justice Cardozo (1934: 383) held that "international law . . . has at times . . . a twilight existence during which it is hardly distinguishable from morality or justice, until at length the *imprimatur* of a court attests its juridicial quality." But for analytical purposes the nature of law, custom, and morality can be distinguished and their respective, contribution to international behavior evaluated.[3]

The first and somewhat elusive difference is in their relative distance from social reality. Custom is nearest to it, almost identical with it. Custom is the usual, prevailing behavior. Customary behavior is regular and predictable. It is stable behavior par excellence. For custom, what is normal becomes norm. The norm may eventually become a legal rule and some law originates from custom—although in the international society the small number of states and precedents makes this a slower process. Societies tend to turn customary into legally obligatory behavior when innovative or deviant behavior disturbs regular behavior patterns. Initially, customary law thus is almost as close to social reality as is custom. It often loses identity with reality because professionals formulate custom as law. It can become even more remote when customary behavior changes but customary law remains in force. Customary law then resembles other types of law in not necessarily corresponding to prevailing practice. This can be the fate of "legislated" law when it tries to be innovative, when it is used as a tool of social change. The law-giving will of men may be creative and attempt to overcome the inertia of the customary. If these men are sufficiently powerful, they may ordain and enforce new modes of behavior. In that case the law may initially be quite removed from prevailing practice and it is the practice that changes to conform with the law. Moral rules may be farthest removed from social reality. The moral rule that men should strive to become perfect is an ideal. It is unrealizable but a signpost for the direction behavior should take.

A second difference, distinguishing custom and law from morality, is the objective, external nature of the first two and the subjective internal nature of the third in regard to their targets. Custom and law aim basically at overt behavior. They are little concerned with the reasons for behavior. They are served when the required behavior is performed. Morality aims at the internal motivation of the actor. It addresses itself to the conscience (which may, of course, be socially conditioned and thereby related to custom). Morality may require a certain behavior, and, when it does, may have an important social function. But it need not. Adultery is overt behavior and can be the object of custom and law. Coveting someone's wife goes beyond overt behavior and can only be the object of a moral rule. Morality addresses itself to the mind and obeying its rules is a satisfaction for the individual. The society is hoping, of course, that moral men cannot but create a moral society. But in principle moral rules are to be obeyed for their own sake. Directly, moral rules aim at achieving stable individuals, while law and custom aim directly at achieving stable societies. The concern of law is the relation between men as social beings. The concern of moral rules is the relation of man to himself. Therefore a person has no legal claim to another on the grounds of moral rules. He has such a claim on the grounds of legal rules and this applies to states as well. States appeal to each other on moral grounds, but they make claims against each other and defend their actions on legal grounds.

This practice may appear to be changing since the birth of so many new states in Asia and Africa. Their leaders more often than others are appealing to moral principles in international relations. For the time being, however, such appeals cannot be more than political weapons, attempts to elicit favorable responses, or, at most, proposals to turn specific moral principles into specific legal rules. The International Court of Justice confirmed in the South-West Africa case (1966: 34) that a court of law "can take account of moral principles only in so far as these are given a sufficient expression in legal form." Moral rules do not turn themselves automatically into legal rules. The distinction between them was made clear and supported at a conference on international law problems in Asia where, according to its rapporteur (Shepherd, 1969: xix), "Some delegates thought that some kind of presumption should exist in favour of the under-developed nations on the grounds of 'international Morality' " to make up for past financial deprivations under colonialism. "This was strenuously resisted by others as subversive of the existing legal order."

Appeals to moral rules have traditionally been made by small or weak states long before the states of Asia and Africa postulated their application. But their legally binding nature has generally been denied. Justice Story (1822: 409), influenced by natural law, argued in the United States v. The Schooner La Jeune Eugénie that "every doctrine, that may be fairly deduced by correct reasoning from the rights and duties of nations, and the nature of moral obligation, may theoretically be said to exist in the law of nations." He declared slave trade illegal on these grounds. A few years later, Chief Justice Marshall (1825: 66), inclining toward positivism, in the case of The Antelope found the trade to be legal. He branded it "contrary to the law of nature" and "abhorrent." Yet, "Whatever may be the answer of a moralist to this question, a jurist must search for its legal solution" and he found it in the uncontested practice of states for over two hundred years. His precedent has been followed ever since (under Cases, see The Créole, 1906: 360). Moral principles can slip into judicial decisions when these are based on equity or on the highly debated principle of the public order *(ordre public)* (see Jenks, 1964: 316-546). They are, of course, also reflected in the law, since law and morality are rooted in the same social value system. But no claim to action can be derived from morality until in some way it becomes part of international law.

The very nature of morality makes its effectiveness in human collectivities altogether questionable. Conscience, the main means of enforcing moral rules, is possessed by individuals, not groups. Moral rules have to be effective through those individuals responsible for the making of decisions and for their execution on behalf of the group. They have occasionally been effective in this way, for instance, when an official resigned rather than compromised moral principles, or when perhaps moral principles played a role in the adoption of the Geneva Conventions on war prisoners and war victims. But their effect is never likely to be as strong as in national societies; one reason is that the individual's behavior is the direct target of the moral rule, but that the decisions for states to act are usually made collectively and any individual's moral responsibility is diluted.

There is, in addition to the problem of the nature of morality in general, also the problem of its particular content, the specific substance of the applicable moral rule. Governments tend to apply different moral rules to relations between states than those prevailing between individuals. In an age of "democratic" foreign policy-making, this practice is not readily admitted; but "my country right or wrong" remains the rule most statesmen will follow and, as a matter of fact, are expected to follow. The consequence is that whatever influence moral rules may have on international behavior caters to national selfishness. Hence the specific rules of morality are not any more conducive to the success of international law; they do not supplement international law any more than morality in general.

The weakness of moral rules in directing social behavior becomes evident also when custom, law, and morality are related to their referents. The obligation of law and the commitment of custom are to a third party. The moral obligation is essentially to the self—at least in the Western and Christian traditions. Accountability for the fulfillment of legal rules is to an outsider (e.g., the government). In denying moral rules, the individual is responsible only to his conscience. This internal, personalized nature of moral rules and their interpretation and application make these rules potentially the least useful for social stability. They may even have a destabilizing effect because the outcome of an individual's obedience to moral rules is unpredictable. There can be as many moralities as there are consciences, and a man's conscience may tell him to disobey a law. No society can therefore ever rely entirely on moral rules. Indeed, those moral rules considered minimally essential for the social order are converted into legal rules (Georg Jellinek's [as quoted in Radbruch, 1910: 9] "ethical minimum"). Clearly, moral rules cannot make a significant contribution to the social order of the international society. This is a regrettable consequence of the manner in which morality functions, for its rules tend to have greater binding force than those of the law. Indeed, in view of the human characteristics opposing restraints on behavior, the question that must be considered is why is law valid and binding at all?

The Binding Force of Law

There are many reasons why law is binding. They range from an assertion that laws are ordained by nature to the belief that law results from the consensus of its subject to be bound. The immediate and simplest answer is that law is binding because men consider it to be. The awareness and consciousness of law by all men serve as the foundation for its existence. Men generally submit their behavior to its regulation, although they may have many different reasons for doing so. Some may believe that in obeying the law they obey the higher authority of the ultimate giver of the law: God, nature, the will of the people. Others acknowledge the content of the law to command obedience. Psychiatrists have argued that men obey the law as an outward reinforcement of an inner compulsion for self-control. Judge Alvarez wrote in the judgment of the Anglo-Norwegian Fisheries case (1951: 148-149): "In the first place, many of the principles, particularly the great principles, have their origin in the legal conscience of peoples (the psychological factor). This conscience results from social and international life; the requirements of this social and international life naturally give rise to certain norms considered necessary to govern the conduct of States inter se."

Most of these reasons raise the further question, however, of why people acknowledge authority or content to be binding, or why they consider norms necessary. For not all people do so with the same intensity or for the same reason, so that in some societies law is more effective than in others, or some laws are more effective than others. The answer must, ultimately, lie in the psychology of men because law aims at influencing their behavior. This again raises the problem of collectivities, which do not have psyches or a behavior as such. No theoretical constructs or legal fictions (e.g., juridical person, corporation, government) can circumvent the fact that law is addressed to individuals who must have reasons for acknowledging or rejecting its binding nature (Kelsen, 1932 IV: 142-144). In collectivities it is a matter of internal arrangements to specify which individuals are responsible for decisions and actions.

One reason for acknowledging the binding nature of law may be, as Aristotle stated, that men are in practice social animals. The survival of individuals in a surviving society becomes the ultimate norm from which the lawmaker derives his authority or from which the content of all other legal norms is derived. This conclusion is based upon the nature of social institutions and the history of social behavior. But it provides no further clue as to which social unit's survival the law is to guarantee: the individual, the state, or the international society? In a world of nation states there can only be little doubt about the supremacy of the state over the individual. Everywhere when survival is at stake the law orders the sacrifice of individuals to the state—though democracy will rationalize this rank order differently from fascism. There can be no doubt at all that the international society ranks at the bottom of the hierarchy. For the evidence is overwhelming in political practice and the international legal system that the welfare of the state precedes that of the international society. The binding force of any rule of international law is therefore likely to be greater the more it provides preferential protection to the state over the international society where the interests of the two are in conflict. Indeed, states create international law to serve their purposes. It is not imposed upon them by some outsider, because there is no outsider. They have no reason, in principle, to disobey their self-created law. Only where more powerful states impose legal rules upon weaker states—as is very often the case—will there be resistance to obedience. Moreover, legal rules are usually sufficiently flexible to be adapted to some changes in the purposes of states.

A second reason for the binding force of law may be that people prefer order over disorder. Women and men are creatures of habit because the habitual way of life requires less personal effort than any other and caters well to a sense of security. Obedience to the law guarantees that way. People also are cautious creatures. Marching in the old grooves is more reassuring than treading new paths. In international politics, especially, deviation from established procedures and precedents can be a matter of life and death for the state. Staying within the framework of international law may reduce the risk of decisions and gives them the legitimacy of previous agreements. Hence the insistence of all states that they are abiding by the law and their appeals to other states to do likewise.

This parsimony—saving effort and risk—as a motivation for obedience to the law may also provide a third reason. It positively pays to follow the law. In orderly societies the social product is cheaper because productivity is greater. The cost of maintaining order is reduced to a minimum. Social energy can be used to improve the society. The growth of orderly, legal relationships in the international society, as shown by the development of international organizations and conferences, seems to indicate that states too have realized the profitability of peaceful, well-regulated contacts. Under modern conditions it is cheaper to trade than to fight and the process, once begun, is self-propelling. More interaction tends to produce interdependence. For international law this means a greater role because the larger the volume of interaction, the greater the need and convenience of legal regulation with a strengthening of its binding force.

A fourth reason for obeying law may be due to the socialization process. People are brought up to obey law. The legal way of life becomes the habitual way of life. There still remains some conscious acquiescence in the legal way so that a modicum of voluntarism essential for dignifying a rule of behavior as law exists. (If compliance were merely due to coercion—"I must act"—there is lacking a sense of obligation—"I ought to act"—which is an indispensable accoutrement of a legal or moral rule.) It is doubtful, however, that the legal socialization process has become so developed in the international society that it could explain legal behavior of states (Gould and Barkun, 1970: 128-129). State behavior is usually deliberate behavior, the habit-forming process of socialization remains more effective for individuals in national societies than for individuals acting on behalf of their states on the international scene.

A fifth reason why law is considered binding has to do with the sense of justice which every man possesses. It guides men's behavior in fulfillment of their wish to see justice prevail in their social relations–whatever their individual interpretation of the concept may be. Law could be one way for translating justice into behavior. Justice therefore becomes one standard by which the quality of law may be measured and respect for it engendered. Obedience to the laws may well be proportionate to the degree to which they satisfy the sense of justice. This relationship can be discovered in the behavior of states as well, although here there is not only the usual difficulty with collectivities, but also an aggravation of the usual difficulty in defining what justice demands and in enforcing the agreement once reached.

The birth of many new states both new and underdeveloped has once more made the problem of justice and its relationship to law very acute. Their standard complaint is the unjust nature of an international law that legalized colonialism and that even now fails to prescribe amends for the consequences or compensations for existing inequalities. Their demand for a "new" international law is justified by them with the need for a better alignment between law and justice. They insist upon distributive justice: reward according to merit and need (e.g., taxation according to ability to pay); and the abandonment of the traditional absolute or corrective justice: strict reciprocity and commutation (e.g., "an eye for an eye").[4] From this conception springs a formulation of rights and obligations, of legal commitments, far removed from that hitherto prevailing among states. Treaties are considered invalid if they are "unequal" and inequality may, for instance, be involved if a treaty is "humiliating" and "injurious," as Panama pointed out in the United Nations General Assembly in complaining about the agreement regarding the Canal Zone (United Nations, 1962c: 113). Aid is demanded as a right. The Charter of Algiers, to name one of innumerable examples, signed by the "Group of 77" underdeveloped nations, in referring to a trend of the rich getting richer and the poor getting poorer, claims that "The international community has an obligation to rectify these unfavorable trends and to create conditions under which all nations can enjoy economic and social well-being . . ." (United Nations, 1967a: 5; see also Hassner, 1964: 40; Schröder, 1970: 61; Darjar, 1960-1961: 276-277). The Yugoslav government proposed for universal acceptance a clause on "sovereign equality" of states which included the rule that states "shall be entitled to every assistance on the part of the international community in making such equality effective, particularly in the economic field" (United Nations, 1964b: 149; see also 1964a: 9-10).

This agitation by some states to bring law more into accord with justice highlights the broader problem that law and justice are not necessarily identical, with the correlated effect upon the binding nature of the law. A discrepancy is not gladly admitted either by governments or by judges. Governments everywhere, even dictatorships, are attempting to develop public agencies through which different principles of action and different systems of values can be brought into accord within widely accepted concepts of justice. Judges and arbitrators in international cases have often—in an earlier era more than today—argued that laws are the legal embodiment of principles of justice. Yet the arbitrament of coercion and force, especially when applied by one of the parties involved, is certainly the least likely way of reconciling justice with law and producing enthusiastic obedience to the law. But this is the ultimate method by which in the international society the issue may be settled. It has produced the dilemma that violence, even if exercised in the name of justice, must be contained before justice can prevail. Lord Halifax, in explaining Great Britain's decision to recognize the Italian conquest of Abyssinia, argued that when two ideals were in conflict—"on the one hand, the ideal of devotion, unflinching but impractical, to some high purpose; on the other, the ideal of a practical victory for peace"—he could not doubt that the stronger claim was for peace (1938: 98). Several makers of the United Nations Charter opted for a reverse order in the solution of this problem. Peace was to be maintained at all costs, except the cost of justice. But when weaponry has become a threat to the survival of mankind it may well be argued, as Julius Stone has, "that first priority in peace enforcement must be for immediate ending of hostilities, without pausing to determine the justice of the parties' cause" (1974: 409).

During the San Francisco Conference on the Charter it was proposed to define the purpose of the United Nations as the maintenance of "international peace, security and justice." But the idea was turned down. The feeling was, reported the rapporteur of Committee I, that to add "justice" was to bring in "at that juncture of the text a notion which lacks in clarity and welds it together with the more clear and almost tangible notion of peace and security." It would open a loophole for questioning any action the organization might wish to take by producing an unending debate over an "abstract definition." The organization should first stop a threat to or breach of the peace. Thereafter "it can find the latitude to apply the principles of justice and international law." The final compromise formulation in the Charter was to maintain peace and security "in conformity with the principles of justice and international law" (Kelsen, 1951: 17, footnote 3). Thus, justice and law remain recognized as separable items. Specific references to the application of justice in settling disputes between states can be found mostly in conventions regarding claims states have against each other and in arbitration treaties. In such agreements awards are to be based upon "equity" and "justice," but even then arbitrators often expressed the view that these bases must also conform to international law.[5]

For the international society, characterized by an extreme and predominant role of power, Blaise Pascal's dictum (Brunschvicg, 1904: 23) might seem particularly applicable that "justice without might is helpless; might without justice is tyrannical." But the danger is not so much that justice will be suppressed by tyranny—at least not for all states. The diffusion of power among many states will prevent at least any one from imposing its law or concept of justice on all. The danger is greater that justice will be flouted altogether and law will then be disobeyed as "unjust." There are two strong reasons for such concern.

The first reason is that distributive justice—if that is to prevail—requires a neutral third party to define what justice is in a given case. There is no such party. The second reason is that all states are willing to have justice prevail mainly for themselves. Their standard of justice is their own interests, in which the welfare of the international society or of any other state may not be included. There is no way of deducing legal rules valid for all states from such a subjectively defined standard. There is only one exception. Rules acknowledging and preserving the supremacy of the national interest will be acceptable to all states. As long as such divisive selfishness represents the substance of international justice it may indeed serve as a source of international law. That it does so in fact is evidenced by the legal principle of sovereignty and its consequences, especially when this principle is interpreted as giving states much freedom to behave as they please. Sovereignty as the most solidly and universally recognized principle of international law when stated in the abstract provides no proof that law is obeyed when it is experienced as just. The reason is that states understand and use sovereignty to find relief from obedience to law (Mander, 1947: 805-814). Under the conditions prevailing in the international society, justice can hardly be counted among the important reasons why states consider law binding, which is to the detriment of the law's effectiveness.

SANCTIONS

Sanctions for disobedience to the law are surely among the reasons why laws have binding force. They assume a special place in a discussion of international law because the argument has been made that the lack of effective sanctions to enforce international law robs international rules of behavior of their legal character. More specifically, the argument has been made that sanctions as an integral part of law distinguish legal from other rules, and that sanctions are coercion following disobedience to the law. The rationalization of this argument has been that while men may acknowledge law to be necessary, they may refuse to obey a particular law because they consider either the maker of the law or its content illegitimate. Yet society cannot afford to let its individual members decide which laws are to be obeyed. The common experience is that therefore governments or some central agency enforce the law and are endowed with an apparatus of coercion for that purpose.

But, in answer to that argument, experience also shows that national legal systems resting mainly upon physical enforcement for their functioning are very ineffective. Moreover, there are laws in national legal systems having no sanctions (e.g., payment of gambling debts cannot be enforced; a new marriage is valid even if the waiting period after the preceding divorce was ignored).

The weakness of the argument is too narrow a definition of sanctions. It is true that especially in international relations physical sanctions are deeply involved in politics and more often than not dysfunctional (see Brown-John, 1975: 3). But there are many other sanctions which are not physical. Any disagreeable consequence following disobedience can be a sanction. It could be a bad conscience, social ostracism, loss of prestige, and a host of others. This applies to the international society as well. Most states are striving for status and rank in the international social order; it is a factor of power. Part of that striving is to be known as a reliable and law-abiding state. The tribunal in the North Atlantic Coast Fisheries arbitration (Scott, 1916: 167) enumerates as sanctions "appeal to public opinion, publication of correspondence, censure by Parliamentary vote, demand for arbitration with the odium attendant on a refusal to arbitrate, rupture of relations, reprisal, etc."

Disobeying the law can have its own self-executing sanction. If the preceding analysis of the reasons for obedience is correct, disobedience would destroy the social order people cherish, would destroy the utility of effective law, would cost an effort in undoing the results of socialization. A law forbidding stealing promotes the social order whether there is a special sanction (other than creating disorder if the rule did not exist) or not. Even the thief considers law binding. He bases his theft on the validity and binding nature of laws regardless of sanction. When he steals money or property he expects that he can obtain the advantages legal ownership or possession confers upon the (mis)appropriated goods. Punishing the thief is an additional law intended to protect the social order. Most sanctions, certainly all government-enforced sanctions, are themselves based upon legal or other rules establishing them. That sanctions alone are powerless to enforce laws is demonstrated by the obsolescence of laws which remain on the books without being applied.

There is undeniably a close relationship between law and sanction. Absence of any sanction, if such a situation were conceivable, might make a society impossible. People may legitimately disagree on what the validity or the content of a law is. On purely technical grounds alone an agreement on such points cannot always be reached, or be reached in time for safeguarding the social order. Some agent must make and enforce a decision. This merely means that sanctions imposed by a third party implement other sanctions, either those internalized by the individual (e.g., moral conscience) or those established in many other social institutions designed to make law binding (e.g., religious duty). But the relationship between law and sanction is not one where sanction is the sine qua non. The effectiveness of law and the effectiveness of sanctions each rest on their own grounds. Furthermore, the possibility that law can exist independently of sanctions is demonstrated by the fact that many legal rules are welcomed by their subjects as useful guidance for desirable behavior. Although laws are always restraints upon behavior, they may not always be experienced as such and require no threat of sanction for their fulfillment. The Acting Chief Justice of Hongkong in the Prometheus case (1906: 224-225) stated that a law remains a law "although it may be impossible to enforce obedience thereto" or because "resistance, perhaps, cannot be overcome."

The examination of the role of sanctions and, earlier, of the other reasons that might explain the binding nature of law indicates that the obligatory nature of law and the effectiveness of the legal system are rooted outside the legal system itself. No legal order could endure without the natural and social guarantees provided by the culture in which it functions. This is merely repeating that law and the legal system are the product of human enterprise. Both are parts of a comprehensive social system whose reality is in the entirety of the relations between the members of the system and whose integration (i.e., what makes it a system, some entity composed of interdependent parts) is in the human beings constituting it. This entire social system provides the contents of all its subsystems, the legal among them, and defines their nature. The system is the ultimate reason for the binding nature of law (see Carr, 1949: 177-180).

Law—The Mirror of Its Society

Effective law has no existence independent of the society which it regulates. Law is a function of the whole society. It does not stand apart from that society nor is it only a part of it. With all social behavior as its subject matter, law penetrates every aspect of the society. It has no material substantive content of its own. As an integral part of a given society, there can be no ideal blueprint of a legal system into which a society could be fitted. The futility of all abstract constitutions for a better world, from biblical days to the present, is witness to that fact.

Normally, the substance of law originates within the interest groups it regulates. Ultimately, it originates in the total culture of the society. Social facts are the material sources. Rules become law as a resultant of social forces generated by all parts of the society. The "legislative process" may be understood in its most comprehensive sense as involving the whole society, with the "legislators" being all participating actively in the creation of the law. Certainly for an understanding of any given law, its functioning, and its efficacy, such a comprehensive approach is most advisable.[6] This is particularly true of the international society where institutional separation of the various steps leading to the creation of law is highly underdeveloped or absent.

Many of the newer states base their attack upon existing (positive) rules of law as outdated on this approach. India, for instance, insisted typically during the Goa debate in the United Nations that she could not accept "colonial law" because "International law is not a static institution. It is developing constantly. If international law would be static, it would be dead driftwood, if it did not respond to the public opinion of the world" (United Nations, 1961b: 17).

Law as a part of a society's culture is at the same time its condensation. The entire culture is broader than can be expressed in the law. And the total process of creating law is broader than the specific institutions (legislatures, administrations, courts) through which the process eventually moves. The law mirrors its culture in minimized form. At the same time, it is also a sediment, a condensed result of the entire norm-creating process.

The "legislative" process, when understood in this comprehensive fashion, encompasses a large number of participants, many arenas of action, and the homogenization of many interests and values. They are all relevant to discovering the meaning of what eventually becomes the law. They can all assist in explaining the efficacy or inefficacy of the law. But for a rule to become a legal rule, there is in all societies a narrowing and formalization of this process toward a more technical procedure. This procedure and its outcome must be the focus in a study of international law. The broader context must be kept in mind for a complete analysis of the law. Indeed, this perspective almost forces itself upon the student of law for mainly two reasons. One is that the validity or adequacy of much existing positive law is being questioned in many quarters, especially the newer and Communist states. The other is that the constant and rapid changes in the international society make the body of rules so far incomplete, and in the inevitable creation of much new law the broader needs and diverse goals of the international society are under constant debate. In brief, the relationship between social policies and the law for their realization is very evident. The law becomes useful therefore not merely as a regulator of social behavior. It also serves as an indicator of the society's condition.

Of course, the law as an abstract and the essence of its society's culture lacks the richness, variety, but also much of the ambiguity and fluidity of a society's culture. As a compensating virtue, perhaps, it represents the basic features of its society in fairly clear and precise fashion. This quality enables the law to render a social service as a means of social communication in addition to defining the commitment to a certain behavior, and it does so in any society.[7] It assists the members of the society to orient themselves about their position in the society and in relation to their fellow members. It also clarifies what the society expects of them and, at least minimally, what they may expect from their society. It symbolizes socially acceptable ideals. In conflict situations, the legal formulation of demands circumscribes and conveys the parties' intentions. It also establishes the limits within which interests may be developed and pursued with any hope of peaceful and orderly satisfaction. The possible disadvantage of legal formulation of social issues is that in defining them the law also sharpens them. Clear definition may highlight a confrontation which previously may have been softened by ambiguities. This byproduct of using the law is at the base of the long debate over the merit of settlement of conflicts by consensus and arbitration rather than by adjudication.

Law can be a means of social communication because it reveals conventional values and orders them in a hierarchy. It becomes a measure of the compromises, adjustments, and agreements a society has achieved. It assists the peacefulness of social change by establishing the rightfulness of existing interests and the conditions of their satisfaction, and by legitimizing the making of future claims and the means for their satisfaction. Contrary to the belief—not erroneous but incomplete—that law tends to conserve existing conditions, it can also facilitate continuing agreement on social problems and the manner of their solution. Where the binding force of law is weak, as in the international society, it remains useful as a means of communication.

Once law as a mirror of its society is recognized, there must also be an awareness that the picture it reflects may be either incomplete or askew. Law can never be coterminous with the entire culture or all the social interaction of its society. Legal rules never reflect social reality completely. More important, occasionally laws may not reflect social reality at all. Eugene Ehrlich (1936: vol. 5) referred to this possibility when he distinguished between positive law—mainly the law on the books—and the "living law"—the actually practiced normative habits, the "normative inner order" of the society. Familiar evidence of such a discrepancy is provided by formally democratic constitutions of totalitarian societies. In the international society, ideals embedded in charters of international organizations (often introduced to appease popular demands) have frequently little relation to the practice of international politics. The possible distance between the reality assumed in the law and the reality of social life is illustrated by Anatole France's saying that the law is just because rich and poor are equally forbidden to sleep under bridges, to beg in the streets, or to steal bread.

There are many reasons for such discrepancies. For one, legislative capacity is limited by the legislator's ability and by the law's inability to reach all aspects of life. Then there are latent forces in every society not included in existing law yet insisting upon expressing themselves. Third, the inevitably abstract formulation of the law provides room for maneuver for its addressees, interpreters, administrators, and indeed, the entire society. Finally, law is made by men holding power not shared by others, or by states superior in power to other states. The law not only expresses power but also serves as a tool of power. The favorable position of the powerful is often not evident, it is disguished, as is shown by the legal and real position of the rich and the poor or by the equal accessibility of the open seas to naval and nonnaval nations. With this caveat regarding the reality of the picture reflected by law, it can be maintained rightly that law most directly reflects the politics and the political system of the society. Its substance and functioning are their resultant. Therefore the admonition of the politician or the lawyer not to mix up politics and law can only be an attempt, usually suspect, by both not be be restrained in the exercise of their particular functions. The two are inseparable, and neither can be understood or properly practiced without regard to the other. This applies to the international society as well where the politician, having the upper hand, tends to suppress the lawyer altogether.

Law and Politics

Law is an instrument of politics. It is intended to perform in its own peculiar manner the maintenance of social order which politics is intended to perform in its peculiar manner. For this reason, law and politics share a number of characteristis. Both, for example, result from human motivations and wills. Both address themselves to behavior–coordinating, adjusting, and regulating it. Both depend in their effectiveness on men's agreement upon their individual and social goals. They also have differences due to the peculiar manner in which they are trying to achieve their purposes. The crucial difference is that politics decides who the lawmaker and what the formulation of the law shall be; law formalizes these decisions and makes them binding. This distribution of functions makes law dependent upon politics.

The political process evaluates and adjudges social issues, social interests, and social behavior. The result of this process is embodied in law. Politics must precede law. The simple reason is that the creation of law is a political act, whoever formally is performing it (the legislature, the judiciary, or any other body defining law). The complex reason is that men through successive generations first choose the conditions of their social existence and thereafter firm their choice in law. Law needs this previous decision on the nature of the order it is to maintain. In the words of Sir Hartley Shawcross (United Nations, 1947a: 7) "history showed that law always follows order and does not precede it." No inherent quality is instructing the law to establish a particular order, for instance, instructing it to protect or forbid private property.

Once law exists, an interaction with politics begins. Politics is not only determining law. Law is also determining politics. The interaction exists because regularity and predictability in the political processes is an indispensable part of social order, hence a function of law. How, for instance, a lawmaker is chosen, what his jurisdiction shall be, and in what manner laws must be made can all be legally defined. In different societies there can be wide differences between the competence of power and that of law. In totalitarian states, despotic régimes, or in any polity using physical coercion as a substitute for law, the competence of power is great, that of law narrow. Arbitrary, unpredictable rule is characteristic of such régimes. There is a resemblance between them and the international polity. Democratic states, a Rechtsstaat, any polity permitting the exercise of power to be regulated in some fashion, are distinguished by legal restraints upon the use of power (and a chance of the judiciary to participate in the development of law).

There are many different reasons why those in power tolerate or establish legal restrictions upon the exercise of their power. They may be subject to the impact of existing social institutions; their power may be limited by the power of those subject to the law; they may be moved by ideals; they may judge their method the most profitable. Their self-limitation is an act of choice—by the holders of power or their predecessors. There appears little need to resort to elaborate fictional constructs to explain the exercise of power, such as the "organic nature" of the state; a "sovereign" beyond, outside, and prior to the state; or "the normativity of the factual." None of these recondite explanations affects or changes the fact that law results from political decisions made by men. Its form, substance, and much of its effectiveness depend greatly upon political power. When many of the newer states reject obedience to parts of international law because it expresses "power politics" they are quite correct about the fact. But if the validity of law would have to depend upon its divorce from politics, there would never be law. What can be done is to create a social system in which the competence of the law is increased and that of power reduced; for it is true, as the newer states imply, that the role power plays in a given society will greatly affect the nature and functioning of its legal system. The unique and domineering role power plays in the international society has much to do with the character and efficacy of international law. What the newer states are presumably trying to say is that the major nations should restrain the exercise of their power so that law has a greater chance to prevail.

Politics and law in performing their functions have different effects due to their different methods. The chronological priority of political decisions over the creation of law means a greater flexibility and adaptability to social change. Law serves primarily to preserve order, although this does not necessarily mean a static social order. It serves to maintain orderly processes, including those of change. However, the prime mover of social change is politics. Only occasionally is law used formally to produce social change, although even then it is likely to be a tool of politics and politicians. An example would be the introduction of a democratic constitution in Japan after World War II, which certainly was a dead letter at the moment of its introduction and which only gradually became living law. More often social needs and social opinions move ahead of the law. The issues they raise are normally settled by political processes and then firmed in laws. In the international society it does indeed happen often that allegedly desired innovations are incorporated in treaties (e.g., the Charter provision for an international police force of the United Nations) but that the implementing political decisions or the requisite political behavior is not forthcoming. Politics tends to be more reflective of social conditions as they are, and is therefore more abreast of social change than is law.

Emerging from this analysis of law in general are points of considerable relevance to an understanding of international law. All law is man-made and part of the social environment men have created for themselves. The nature of the society can help explain the nature of its law. In particular, the dependence of law upon the society's politics makes the political system the determinant of the legal system and the content of law. As human products, politics and law are directly and fundamentally related to the motivations, sentiments, attitudes, and interests of the men making up the society. The character of the law and the functioning of the legal system can only be analyzed by continual reference to the society in which they exist and to the human factors which define the nature of any given society. In this study, which is aiming at an analysis of why international law is what it is rather than of what it ought to be, international law will be examined in the context of the international society and its human foundation, more particularly in the context of the society's politics.

The topics to be investigated in the following chapters therefore are:

(1) Can there be law when states consider themselves sovereign and independent?

(2) Have states succeeded in maintaining themselves the exclusive, sovereign subjects of international law?

(3) Can there be international law in the face of very uneven sets of relationships between states?

(4) How can law prevail when its subjects are highly unequal and insist on maintaining and exploiting this inequality?

(5) With so many different cultures existing in the international society is there a common ground for the validity of law?

(6) In view of the predominance of power in the social system of the international society, how can law fulfill the function of regulating state behavior?

(7) What may be the effect of the nationalist approach people everywhere take toward the international society upon the nature and efficacy of international law?

After a discussion of these questions, it will be profitable to apply its results to some of the specific aspects of concrete international law: its sources; its contribution to international cooperation; and to the settlement of international conflicts. In brief, it will be profitable to examine to what extent international law produces an orderly international society.

NOTES

1. A law is efficacious when it produces the desired behavior mandated or authorized toward the social order (Jones, 1969: 3-4).

2. For a more detailed analysis, see Levi (1974a: 64-66, and Carr (1949: 182-187).

3. For details on the distinction between custom, law, and morality, see Radbruch (1932: 36-49), Geiger (1964: 169-204, 293-336), Tucker (1966: 570-571), D'Amato (1971: 26-31), Waldock (1963: 68-70), also Landheer (1957 I: 44-61).

4. For a discussion of this difference as it applies to international law, see Dillard (1957 I: 549-550), also Wright (1959 III: 130-134), Nef (1941: passim), Dégan (1970: 97-107). A survey of the attitude of "new" states on international law and of the literature on that subject can be found in Udokang (1971).

5. For many examples, see Jenks (1964: 330-357). Article 7 of the Hague Convention XII of 1907 relating to an International Prize Court, which never came into existence, provided that in the absence of treaty provisions or rules of international law, decisions shall be made "in accordance with the general principles of justice and equity." See also Schwarzenberger (1962: 13, 18-19).

6. This approach has been developed in detail by Myres McDougal and Harold Lasswell and has been formed into a system. Their views can be found in many of their writings, especially those of McDougal. On the point made in the text, see McDougal, Lasswell, and Reisman (1967). Cf. also Higgins (1968). For an introduction to McDougal and Lasswell's jurisprudence, see Moore (1972: 42-76). Cf. also Grewe (1970: 371).

7. On law as a means of social communication, see Arnold (1962: 33-38), Coplin (1966: 1-2), Falk (1965: 237-238), Gould and Barkun (1970: 136-149), Ostrower (1965: vol. 2, 713-729), Stone (1959: xliii-xliv); see also the statement by the Philippino delegate, Teodoro Evangelista that "clear and definite statements of the principles of international law would alleviate the tension in international affairs" (United Nations, 1947b: 12).

Chapter 2

NATIONAL SOVEREIGNTY AND INTERNATIONAL LAW

The international society, as a human organization, is based upon and conditioned by the interests, motivations, and capabilities of the people composing it. They determine the character of the international society. In particular, they are responsible for the changes in the nature of that society as well as for the differences between the national and the international societies. The subjective, human foundation of the national and the international societies is at the root of two types of different social units, one embodied in the nation, the other in the international society. The first is a community. The other, for want of a better name, is a society in the narrower sense, or perhaps an association. The distinction, somewhat out of fashion now, was first worked out in detail by Ferdinand Tönnies (1935), and is well designated by the German terms *Gemeinschaft* and *Gesellschaft.* There are resemblances between the two, but they also have partly different structures and institutions. More important is that the crucial difference is in the different attitudes underlying the two units. They explain the different functioning of even outwardly comparable institutions, including the legal system and the law.[1]

Society, Community, and Law

The society is the more loosely structured group. Its members are joined for the performance of functions. The society has the instrumental value of bringing them together and organizing them for the achievement of some ulterior purpose to which the society is incidental. It rests upon the function nexus of its members. The quality of the society concerns them mainly as a means to reach their individual ends. If their ends can be reached without or against the society, they would lose their interest in maintaining the society. In principle, the society would disappear with the fulfillment of the purposes it is organized to achieve.

The community is the more closely knit group. Its archetype is the family. But it can be expanded to the size of a nation. Its members also perform functions together. The community can have an instrumental value to achieve some purposes. But additionally, the members also have an emotional investment in the community. They are tied to it (or to each other) by bonds of sentiment and solidarity. They identify with the community and derive considerable psychic satisfaction from membership. The community thus possesses an inherent value for its members. In the case of the nation, the national community is the highest social value of the citizen. The functions joining the members of a society are supplemented in a community by the addition of sentimental satisfactions. The members are therefore concerned with the quality of the community for its own sake. Their dual interest in its existence would allow a community to continue its existence even if it failed to achieve its ulterior, functional purpose.

The different psychic foundations of the two collectivities become socially relevant when they appear objectified in different institutions. The behavior of the members—whether organized as citizens of a state, or the people of a nation—will differ, if not outwardly, then certainly in motivation. The law is affected possibly in its content and in any case in its effectiveness. Generally, community law will foster the community and superordinate it to other social collectivities. Society law will foster the society only to the extent that it becomes a good instrument for the achievement of ulterior purposes. The burden upon the law will be lighter in the community because the community is cherished, the society merely useful. Community members tend to accept restraints upon behavior more readily as welcome guides for the improvement of the community. Selfish interests of the community members may include the community's welfare and not hinder the social function of the law. Selfish interests of a society's members may have the opposite effect if there is no identity between the member's and the collectivity's interests. Undermining a society is undermining merely a means to an end; undermining a community is undermining an end itself. The law, in brief, will be more effective in a community than in a society. The different character, functioning, and efficacies of national and international law and their respective legal systems will become more readily understandable when they are examined in the light of these different psychic foundations.

Sovereignty and Law

The sentiments invested in the national community are expressed as nationalism. The institution making nationalism politically and legally operational is sovereignty. It is the major characteristic distinguishing the international from the national society. It means, in the words of Arbitrator Max Huber (Scott, 1932: 92), "independence." It signifies in the political and legal sphere the people's insistence that their state shall be supreme and its individuality inviolate.

A state is politically sovereign when there is no higher authority directing its behavior, when it is free to make its own political decisions. Whether, in fact, a state has such freedom is very difficult to discover because it is nearly impossible to find out what influences affect its decisions. The concept is increasingly murky as interaction and interdependence between states grow. The mutual sensitivities among states allow only for varying degrees of independence. Nevertheless, the demand for independence everywhere is responsible for the organization of the international society, informing its institutions, including law, all designed to give substance to the demand.

Legal sovereignty seems to be more easily definable, perhaps, because the language of law is more precise than that of politics. However, the fact of legal sovereignty is hardly more easily ascertainable. It could be purely nominal sovereignty. This is the case when a defeated nation signs a peace treaty. But as long as the state acquires rights and enters into obligations formally through its government, legal sovereignty is preserved.

Political sovereignty is continuously being fought out in the political arena as states strive to preserve their independence. Legal sovereignty is more often debated by international lawyers. The problem they feel confronts them is that a state's submission to international law may not readily be reconcilable with legal sovereignty.

The practitioners of politics have the smaller problem. Everybody is aware that sovereignty in the sense of absolute independence cannot be had for states any more than for citizens within a state. It is always a question of more or less. Politicians look for pragmatic solutions, trying to enlarge independence and to diminish obligation.

In the legal arena the requirement is to be logical, specific, and hard. The purpose of the law can be fulfilled the better the more certain it is. In principle, at least, it cannot leave the relationship between independence and obligation undefined, nebulous, or variable—although international law often does exactly that. In practice, such a condition appeals to governments in the hope that it will enable them to enlarge their state's independence by political means. It also nourishes their cherished illusion that they are independent and enter into commitments on their own free will. International lawyers have therefore developed for hundreds of years theories respectful of reality, permitting people to believe that their sovereignty has been preserved even while subjecting their states to international law.[2]

The weakest theory probably is that sovereignty permits a state to bind itself on its own volition. But if it can do that, it can as easily unbind itself. Nothing is gained for the obligatory nature of international law. Most of the other theories rest on faith or belief. One states that one legal order prevails in the world of which international and national law are subdivisions. Another asserts that, objectively, generally valid legal principles exist, independent of human choice, binding all human beings. A variant of this theory maintains that regardless of legal principles rationality instructs people to acknowledge equality and corresponding mutual treatment as an inevitable requirement of their association.

Once the theoretical problem of sovereignty in priniciple has been solved, detailed questions arise and theorizing continues about whether, for instance, sovereignty is divisible between a state's internal and external independence or in regard to subject matter; or whether sovereignty exists prior to the rise of international law or is its consequence. Much of the substance of such problems lies within jurisprudence and has little relevance to the relation between politics and law.

SOVEREIGNTY AND LAW IN PRACTICE

The theory of relative legal sovereignty is favored here (following Verdross, 1964: 8). A state is subject to international law, but not to the law of any other state. This position was well formulated by Dionisio Anzilotti, as judge of the Permanent Court of International Justice in the case of the Customs Régime between Germany and Austria (see under Cases, 1931: 58). Sovereignty can be lost only, he decided, in a relationship of superiority and inferiority between states, namely, when one state is "legally compelled" to submit to the will of another state. "Where there is no such relation . . . it is impossible to speak of dependence within the meaning of international law. It follows that the legal conception of independence has nothing to do with a State's subordination to international law." This is, of course, an opinion or assertion. But it takes account of the inevitable subjection of states to some rules of social order, while not overly offending logic by also granting them their legal sovereignty up to a point. It does not answer all the questions that can be raised, but it is parsimonious and reasonably responsive to reality. It is, at any rate, not in conflict with the first Principle of the United Nations obliging all members to respect the "sovereign equality" of states.

Neither statesmen nor peoples are greatly worried over possible inconsistencies between sovereign independence and subjection to international law. They refer to both and, more important, insist upon both. States agree that they are sovereign and that they are bound by international law. The General Assembly of the United Nations, for instance, resolved in 1960 that states have the "sovereign right" to dispose of their natural wealth, but "in conformity with the rights and duties of States under international law." It resolved again, in 1962 that a state can take measures relating to its natural wealth "in the exercise of its sovereignty and in accordance with international law" (see United Nations General Assembly Resolution, 1960a; 1962).

Evidently, in shaping their international society, men have no difficulty in reconciling what may logically be incompatibles. They can make their states sovereign, just as, by accession or merger, they can make them disappear. The international social organization they have created, and the law that supports it, have made sovereignty as well as obedience to international law a practical possibility. But it is a limited possibility. The extent of independence and the extent of obligation vary, depending upon how much states need each other.

At the time sovereignty developed into its most extreme form—which remains largely reflected in international law—the wish for national independence was not utopian. States were largely self-supporting in the basic requirements of their populations. Interaction was limited. Internal affairs were indeed mostly internal; international relations were often luxuries. Sovereignty performed some useful functions. It contributed to the international social order at a time when social change threatened to upset established routines and institutions. It identified international actors and categorized international action. The cost of sovereignty was low and the psychic satisfaction it provided was high. Its feasibility became questionable mainly after an enormous increase in the volume of international interaction.

International Society Versus National Community

Social coexistence under the conditions of voluminous interaction obviously requires a different behavior by states than was required in the heyday of sovereignty. The necessary limitations upon the freedom of national action are not easily conceded by a surviving nationalism. It resists the growth of legal regulations and controls which inevitably accompany increasing interaction. The division of labor among states, the subsequent mutual sensitivities among them, and the development of the world into one action area (Lasswell) inexorably lead to diminishing independence and augmenting international law. Much subject matter formerly protected by sovereignty or not existing at all (such as freedom of the air, protection of the biosphere) becomes internationalized and subject to international regulation.

"Pollyannic" theories that obligations entered into voluntarily by states are an attribute, not a restriction, of sovereignty become more unconvincing as more subject matter becomes internationalized.[3] With increasing rapidity as technology advances, the substance of sovereignty is thinning while the body of legal rules is fattening. Foreseeably the major function of sovereignty could be to satisfy the nationalist citizen's emotional attachment to his national community, until even that sentiment is eroded by the conditions of international coexistence. Gradually the awareness of international judges and arbitrators will become general "how largely the increase of civilization, intercourse, and interdependence as between nations has influenced and moderated the exaggerated conception of national sovereignty" and that it is an "undeniable fact" that the recent tendency of promoting "the common welfare of the international community" has meant "a corresponding restriction of the sovereign power of individual States" (North American Dredging Company of Texas case [United States v. Mexico], 1970: 633; Reservations to the Convention on Genocide, 1951: 46; United Nations, 1949: 39).

Situations occur, however, when the issue cannot be glossed over, when the issue becomes openly acute as a principle, and a solution has to be found. Such situations are experienced as unpleasant by many people because they highlight the dissonance between their devotion to the national community's sovereignty and to the incompatible requirements—as they conceive them—of an orderly international society. A striking example of such a situation, involving not just the more frequent political but also legal problems, was the Soviet Union's interference in 1968 in Czechoslovakia's internal affairs. This intervention was dignified as the new "Brezhnev Doctrine" of limited sovereignty. It declared that Czech independence could be tolerated only as a socialist state. S. Kovalyov, a Soviet international lawyer, amplified that sovereignty could not be used to oppose the interests of world socialism and the revolutionary world movement. The Chinese Communists labelled the intervention "Great Power chauvinism." They insisted that sovereignty demanded staying out of the internal affairs of all other states (Erickson, 1972: 52-53; Hsiung, 1972: 74-75; Kaminski, 1973: 206).

Other situations of conflict between sovereignty and legal obligation become openly acute when a compromise between the two has to be achieved. This was the case during the writing of the United Nations Charter. The proposal to introduce the principle of "sovereign equality" was opposed on the ground that sovereignty was an undefinable and hypocritical concept. Because the majority favored the concept, the fairly meaningless agreement was reached to specify that it included "among other things" legal equality of states, respect for a state's "personality" and its right to enjoy the benefits of sovereignty, and a state's obligation to fulfill its duty (Kelsen, 1951: 51).

A similar situation prevailed in the United Nation's Special Committee on Principles of International Law Concerning Friendly Relations and Cooperation Among States. Far-reaching agreement on the desirability of sovereignty was matched by far-reaching disagreement on its meaning. A note was sounded not previously heard from governments. The Czech delegate proclaimed an implied limit to the exercise of sovereignty. It should not "imperil common vital interests of the international community" (United Nations, 1964c: 5). The delegate of the United Arab Republic (United Nations, 1966v: 6) referred to the "common interests of the international community as a whole," as did his Yugoslav, Lebanese, and other colleagues (United Nations, 1966z: 7; 1966w: 14). Over a decade earlier, justices of the International Court were working with this idea.[4]

These references to the interests of the international society were symptomatic of a shift in what is truly within a nation's and the international society's bailiwick. The attempt of all peoples to save a maximum of their illusion and remaining reality of sovereignty from the encroachment of essential international interaction is a losing battle. Devotion to sovereignty has not prevented governments from enlarging the volume of interaction because there is no other way of obtaining the amenities people demand. The transformation of "political" into "welfare" states everywhere under modern conditions irresistibly leads to mutual dependence. International law as one of the regulators of the emerging interrelationships cannot but reflect these changes.

The Changing International Society and Its Law

The basic change taking place is the attempt of international law to protect sovereignty through cooperation among states rather than through their separation. In the past, law sought to preserve national individuality and identity by emphasizing what states must not do to each other, and respectively, what they were entitled to do against other states to protect their "personality." Law has therefore been preoccupied with territory, borderlines, physical violence, succession, and similar items geared to supreme independence and identity of the state. They retain importance in law because states endow them with importance in politics. This separative spirit of international law expressing divisive nationalism is ill-fitted to the cooperation required for the satisfaction of even selfish concerns of states. A highly refined division of labor across the globe and a great diversification in the interests of states, even their very security, make independent, isolated action by states inadequate. Old and certainly new needs are poorly catered to by traditional international law. Changing relationships among states require the implementation of traditional law with new rules and regulations more adapted to the new realities of international life (see Friedmann, 1964).

The isolated state is gradually giving way to the cooperative state. Cooperation among states is being added, slowly and in scattered but specific ways, as an obligation to the separation of states. Judge Alvarez pointed out in the Ambatielos case (1952: 128) that matters formerly protected as domestic affairs under sovereignty are now subject to "total or partial internationalization."[5] More and more treaty law is binding states in bilateral relationships or in international organizations to cooperative action. The evidence abounds.

Members of the United Nations are committed by the Charter to "develop friendly relations," to "achieve international cooperation," and to "harmonize" their actions. In numerous resolutions (e.g., 1505 [XV] and 1803 [XVI]; see 1960b and 1962) the General Assembly emphasized the duty to cooperate and opened up new areas for such cooperation. Preambles to international agreements and international policy statements refer to commitments to human rights, civil rights, and better living standards.

Contemporary terminology reflects the new approach in concepts as coexistence, union, integration, common market, mutual aid, and interdependence. The United Nations accepted the principle that astronauts shall be regarded as "envoys of mankind in outer space" and speaks of ocean resources as man's common heritage.

States further the trend, often only in the abstract and often for selfish reasons (when cooperation becomes synonymous with aid). Sometimes they speak of it with anxiety, lest cooperation erode sovereignty. But it is *le bon ton* to favor it. A psychological factor enters, as Judge Alvarez implied, when he remarked in the Reservations to the Convention on Genocide case (1951: 53) that states are unwilling to remain aloof from this trend because "if they did so, they would find themselves in an awkward position in the international society." The apparent public pressure to pay at least lip service to the idea of cooperation is a change from the times when national independence rather than international cooperation was the major theme of an international law.

The United Nations Special Committee on Principles of International Law Concerning Friendly Relations and Cooperation Among States was a good place to discover the feelings of governments about the trend. Consensus was expressed by the delegate from the United Arab Republic when he referred to the almost inevitable pressure toward cooperation. He did not think, he qualified, increasing cooperation was entirely voluntary. Rather, it was an adjustment "to existing patterns and requirements" of international relations and the growth of common interests in the international society. The Canadian delegate, with support from his colleagues from Dahomey and other areas, drew attention to the change since the League of Nations days when the emphasis was upon the prevention of conflict whereas today it was upon cooperation for the preservation of peace. By the time the Committee adjourned the view was widespread that cooperation among states was no longer merely a moral or political concept but "part of international law" and "one of the most significant norms of contemporary international law." The principles of cooperation and sharing, jubilated the delegate from Ghana, were gradually replacing those of greed and competition. The delegate from Madagascar christened the new obligation to cooperate the "new law of social interdependence."[6]

In this state of bliss, the demands and concerns of the national community were not forgotten. The urge to make international cooperation a legal obligation stemmed more from reluctantly admitted necessity or anticipated advantages by the developing states than from an inspiring sense of universal brotherhood. The larger, older states worried about the generality of the concept "cooperation" and were wondering what and how much they might have to share with others in its name. Some smaller and newer states, hoping to gain from cooperation, were nevertheless insisting that it must not be subject to political or economic conditions "jeopardizing the sovereign equality of States." Cooperation should be formulated to include the principles of sovereignty, suggested the Yugoslav delegate with general approval. But, summarized the Committee's rapporteur at one point, sovereignty was "conditioned by the concept of equality within a new form of diplomacy based on collective security and co-operation." To what extent cooperation had become a legal obligation was a matter of great uncertainty. A majority of delegates maintained that the principle had legal force when it was embedded in a treaty. But there was no agreement on whether then the principle as such was legally binding, whether it was binding after implementing details had been worked out, or whether it was committing states to some specific behavior (United Nations, 1966z: 6; 1964b: 151).

This advocacy of international cooperation as a legal obligation, mainly by the smaller, newer states, was at worst a ruse by which they hoped to gain political and economic advantages. At best it was an adjustment to new objective conditions with mixed feelings. Whatever concession to cooperation was advocated, it was not to be made at the expense of sovereignty and the body of traditional legal rules protecting it.[7] Interest in the sovereign existence of states retains priority over interest in the international order. The peoples of the world remain attached emotionally to their national communities. The international society remains a loose association; international law continues to reflect these values. Clashing interests in the international society are settled in conflicts unmitigated by the bonds of community softening conflicts within nations.

There may be differences in the zeal with which governments pursue the goal of national independence (in any case not because some would be willing to abandon it, but because some take its existence more for granted than others). But the universally accepted institution of sovereignty and the law that supports it make the international society unique. Nowhere else do members of a society, whether as individuals or as juristic persons, claim total independence from each other. Nowhere else do they presume, as states do, to determine unilaterally and autonomously the conditions of their coexistence. In recognition of the need for social controls and social decisions of public issues they maintain common institutions to organize and maintain their societies, which they endow with power to prevail over individual deviants. Under the régime of national sovereignty common institutions for the authoritative, binding regulation of social order are either absent or underdeveloped. The performance of these institutional (usually governmental) functions is diffused across the international society. This horizontal organization for reaching and executing social decisions places a premium on a state's ability to make its will prevail if necessary. The foundation of the social order is precarious because its instruments are unsuitable (e.g., political power remains in the hands of individual members) or lack in efficacy (e.g., the law). This organization of the international society with its deleterious consequences for its peace and order will remain as long as it is based on two assumptions: that the maintenance of nations is more valuable than the maintenance of the international society; and that the welfare of nations does not necessarily require the welfare of the international society.

NOTES

1. The effect of these differences on international law is discussed by Schwarzenberger (1962: 9-42) and Corbett (1951: 51); see also Durkheim's discussion of law in his *The Division of Labor in Society;* and Gurvitch (1953).

2. Surveys of theories can be found in Waldock (1963: 7-16), Tucker, (1966: 189-194), and Kelsen (1960: 9-100). See also United Nations (1966: 5, 13; 1966d: 5, 10, 11; 1966e: 7-8) for examples from practice.

3. In the Wimbledon case (1923: 25) the Permanent Court of International Justice decided that the right to conclude treaties is an attribute, not a restriction, of sovereignty. A similar conclusion was reached by Judge Reid in the Ambatielos case (1952: 142).

4. See, for instance, Reservations to the Convention on Genocide case (1951: 128) and the Anglo-Norwegian Fisheries case (1951: 152).

5. This development has first been elaborated by Max Huber (1910). It has since been discussed by Wilfred Jenks, Wolfgang Friedmann, and Richard Falk in many of their writings.

6. Judge Alvarez had many years earlier spoken of "the law of social interdependence" in a dissenting opinion in the Ambatielos case (1952: 128). The examples of the discussions taking place in the Special Committee can be found in United Nations (1966v: 6; 1966w: 12, 10; 1966x: 5-6, 7, 8; 1966y: 3).

7. The positions taken by many states at the Law of the Sea conferences are filled with the dilemmas bedevilling states eager to maintain their protection under sovereignty and at the same time to retain established rights or to share in resources located within the sovereign domain of maritime states. Those states in whose jurisdiction straits or resources were located were naturally sensitive about any infringement upon sovereignty. The other states suggested restrictions upon sovereignty in the high-sounding name of "international social justice and equity" or in "the overriding interest of the entire international community." Good illustrations may be found in the general statements at the opening of the Caracas Third United Nations Conference on the Law of the Sea from June 2 to August 29, 1974 (United Nations, 1974c).

Chapter 3

POLITICAL POWER AND INTERNATIONAL LAW

The horizontal organization of politics and political processes in the international society means, negatively, the absence of a central government. Positively, it means the diffusion of making social decisions, of their execution, and of political power among all states. Within states political processes are integrated functionally and hierarchically, with the government at the apex. This ordering is possible because the interests managed by politics are also hierarchical, with the welfare of the national community at the apex. (This welfare is obviously not synonymous with the welfare of every citizen.) In the international society the diffusion of political processes and power corresponds to the diffusion of interests, all of which are individual national interests. Each state must therefore perform the functions normally performed within states by a government. No common international interest subordinates or consistently coordinates the national interests. Each state takes care of its own interests and must possess the means to do so. This necessity exists even in the case of collective goods and "the common heritage of mankind." The handling of such matters imposes severe limitations upon national action and forces states to cooperate. But the conception in the minds of governments remains that such cooperation represents an international pursuit of national interests (otherwise supranational agencies would come into existence).

Experience teaches that on many occasions national interests of different states do not clash sufficiently or are sufficiently complementary and in balance so that all parties find benefit in satisfying them in an orderly, peaceful manner. Indeed, by sheer volume the largest part of international relations is routine and well regulated (but insufficiently impressive to shape the nature of the international system). The exercise of power, that is, the attempt of each state to influence the actions of the others, will be at a minimum and relatively harmless tools will be used. The law under such circumstances can play a welcome and significant role.

Experiencs also teaches, however, that national interests may clash so much that their adequate satisfaction by orderly, peaceful means is difficult or sometimes impossible. In such a situation, power becomes a very prominent factor. The application of power by each state determines, as a rule, the outcome of the conflict of interests. Law is, at best, relegated into the background.

There are in this interplay between law and power similarities between the international and national situations. But there also is an important difference. The power available to the citizen and the manner of its use are defined by his government which, to make such a definition enforceable, has been endowed with a power potential greater than that possessed by any one or by any group of the citizens. Such an arrangement is acceptable because and as long as enough citizens feel that their government is exercising its power more or less for the common welfare. In part, such acceptance is expressed by obedience to the law.

In the international society, in the absence of an acknowledged common welfare, each state caters to its own needs and must have a power potential for doing so. Power is exclusively possessed and exercised by states, an arrangement which the law sanctions through sovereignty. There is no authority above the states either for limiting their power potential or for regulating the manner of its use. Such limitation and regulation are matters of agreement among states and enforceable only by each individually.

This arrangement gives power a totally different role, or at least makes the power factor considerably more important. Essentially and simply, states must be preoccupied with building up a power potential as a significant and in some cases vital guarantee of their very existence. Several consequences arise for international law. The first is that states are not likely to accept laws in the first place which will prevent them from developing the power potential they consider necessary. The second is that as soon as states experience legal commitments as a hindrance in the fulfillment of important national interests, they will seek a release or escape from them. The third is that the costliness of building a power potential, the inability of many states to develop a power potential at all, or the effort of mobilizing an existing potential will lead states into attempts to restrain the role of power. The fourth is that the nature of power and of the international society diminishes the chances for such restraint. These consequences and their effect upon international law will now be examined.

The Struggle for Power

When a political decision is to be made about which state is to get what, when, and how, a trial of power is normally involved because there is no other way of discovering which state has the superior power to obtain a favorable decision. When there is conflict, the interests of the state with a preponderance of power prevail. Hence the enormous incentive for states to develop a power potential. Its elements are legion because influence can be exerted in a number of ways. What elements of its power potential a state will employ in the pursuit of its interests—whether, for instance, persuasion or violence—will depend upon the importance assigned to the interests, upon how much the conflicting interests may be matched by shared interests, and a host of other mostly subjective considerations. This is exactly the situation making the possession of a power potential vital. No state can ever predict with certainty when it may want to mobilize its power or how much of it, either to enforce its own political decision or to resist the enforcement of another state's decision.

This uncertainty is enhanced by the additional uncertainty regarding the magnitude of the power potential and its possible effectiveness. The reason for this lies in the manner in which power achieves its results. Power is a psychological relationship. Each government is trying to influence the other to act in a certain manner. The minds of those responsible for the behavior of a state are the targets of the application of power. What their reaction will be is generally unpredictable and the applied power cannot be measured. Moreover, several elements of power are also unmeasurable, such as the stamina or morale of a people, the prestige of a nation, and the effectiveness of a weapon. Governments can never be sure how much effective power is at their disposal to enforce or oppose decisions. The temptation and, indeed, the tendency are to "maximize" the power potential within the limits of a state's will and capacity. But as power cannot be measured the "maximum" cannot be determined. The enterprise can only mean adding forever increment upon increment of something states hope will increase their power potential. Thus the competition and struggle for power become prominent activities in international politics.

The effect of this situation upon international law is impressive —whatever one's theory is regarding the role of power in international politics. Inevitably under the conditions of the international society all states must be in quest of some power potential and international law is affected thereby, mainly unfavorably.

This quest for power and the application of power may take place within the legal framework. Ethical convictions of a government—genuine or pretended—may, for example, keep them there. Obedience to law can improve a state's reputation, and a good reputation is itself an element in the power potential. But states also use their power for unilaterally making and enforcing their interpretation of the law or for altogether extra- or illegal purposes. They can do so owing to the manner in which they have organized the (non)management of power. They will use it so when they judge the defense of the national interest to require an extra-legal use, although they may well be apologetic or defensive about such practice. For states prefer to remain within the legal framework but also, to facilitate this endeavor, to subject themselves to as few legal restraints as possible.

This wish of states to behave legally, on the one hand, and the need under all circumstances to build a power potential, on the other hand, leads states to keep the volume of legal rules low. They are quick to interpret every legal restraint upon building a power potential as an inhibition of their self-protection, and every restraint upon applying it as a virtual invitation to national suicide. There are situations when states feel more secure by relying upon their own power potential than upon the obedience to law by other states. They want to preserve their freedom to apply their power especially in such situations, and of necessity therefore to develop their power potential.

The connection between the quest for power and international law could appear at first sight to affect only that segment of a state's behavior devoted to building a power potential. But the elements of the power potential are legion, so that this segment becomes practically coterminous with the international behavior of states. There is hardly a limit to the items useful in "power politics" so that everything–things and actions, ideas and processes–can add to the power potential. Almost everything at some point can be useful for one state to influence the behavior of another. Virtually everything can become part of the state's power potential, from an atom bomb to a ping-pong team. Governments therefore routinely scrutinize everything for its relevance to the power potential–even though power may not be the obsessive concern of a particular government. This approach also affects international law.

States are reluctant to commit themselves. They are hesitant to grant legally binding force to general resolutions of international organizations or to be bound to broad concepts such as "international cooperation." The Australian government stated the principle typically when it declared that "a General Assembly declaration of legal principles cannot itself be creative of legal duties" (Friedmann et al., 1969: 98). Once they bind themselves, they are inclined to define their obligations as narrowly as possible. International tribunals have consistently held that when there is doubt about the meaning of a treaty "that interpretation should be adopted which is the most favorable to the freedom of States.[1] The "domestic affairs" or "internal affairs" clause has consistently been used by states to withhold much subject matter from international jurisdiction (see, e.g., United Nations, 1954: 453-478). This limitation has been broadened by the "Connally Amendment." This amendment introduced a reservation when the United

States accepted the so-called compulsory jurisdiction of the International Court of Justice. It stipulated that disputes were excluded relating to matters essentially within the domestic jurisdiction of the United States "as determined by the United States of America." Not only has this reservation been adopted by many other states, but as a type of "subjective" formulation it has also been introduced to narrow many other kinds of international obligations.[2]

Generally, the wish to reserve freedom of action encourages "political" behavior, by which states understand behavior controlled essentially by power relationships. It discourages "legal" behavior, by which they understand behavior in conformity with pre-established rules, making their respective power potential in theory irrelevant. The net effect is to reduce the area of behavior subject to legal controls.

Power Versus Legal Control

The ambivalent attitude of states toward behavior within the law and freedom for accumulating and applying power has produced their practice of building into the body of law rules allowing them to escape legitimately from the bonds of law into the freedom of "political" behavior. Sovereignty is, of course, the main exit from obligatory behavior. But there are many smaller exits as well. The main function of these releases from legal obligation is to prevent binding the behavior of states beyond what they may consider nonessential to their own existence. The dilemma is the wish to tame power but also to exercise it. It has been solved, rather unsatisfactorily, by making the release not so easy as to threaten anarchy in the society, yet easy enough to serve the purpose. In general, the arrangements for limiting legal obligations have been vaguely defined and their use has been made sufficiently risky for social order to make states hesitant in taking advantage of them.

One of these arrangements is the classic "national honor and vital interests" clause. It was in vogue until about 1928. It could be found mostly in arbitration treaties for the exemption of disputes touching the vital interests of a state—if one of the parties made such a claim. In such a case the dispute was to be solved politically, i.e., by a trial of power.

In more recent practice, states distinguish between "legal," hence "justiciable" disputes, and "political," hence "nonjusticiable" disputes. States feeling that the settlement of a dispute by means of their power potential would be of advantage will try to evade any settlement on the basis of law by declaring a dispute political. The distinction between the two types of disputes has been recognized by the International Court. It can also be found in numerous treaties. Most prominent among these is the Locarno Pact of 1925 in which the parties agree to submit to judicial decision all questions "as to their respective rights"; and the United Nations Charter which, in Article 36, instructs the Security Council to refer "legal disputes" as a rule to the International Court of Justice.[3]

The same distinction has now been introduced also in regard to treaties (see Lauterpacht, annual, 1957: 462; de Visscher, 1968: 145-153, 266-269; Henkin, 1965 I: 206-207). The Constitution of the German Federal Republic refers to "political" treaties. The German Federal Constitutional Court declared these to be treaties dealing with public affairs, the good of the community, or affairs of state, and in addition, affecting directly "the existence of the State, its territorial integrity, its independence and its position or relative weight within the community of States." As examples the Court mentioned alliances, treaties of guarantee, peace treaties, treaties relating to political cooperation, and treaties of neutrality and disarmament (Lauterpacht, annual, 1957: 462). The assumption is that such treaties can be more readily opened for renegotiation than other treaties (McNair, 1961: 501-502; Tucker, 1966: 457-458).

A novel and unambiguous release from a treaty obligation was introduced by the United States and the Soviet Union in their Nuclear Atmospheric Test Ban Treaty of 1963. "Each Party shall in exercising its national sovereignty have the right to withdraw from the Treaty if it decides that extraordinary events, relating to the subject matter of this Treaty, have jeopardized the supreme interests of its country."

A very rare, old, and dubious arrangement is the unilateral declaration by a state of a "state of necessity." It can exist when the vital interests or the existence of a country are at stake. It differs from the concept of legitimate self-defense and of military necessity in that the state of necessity need not be brought about by an illegal act of some other country. For instance, a country whose population is starving could seize a foreign ship loaded with foodstuffs and give this act legality by claiming a state of necessity. The principle is that a country, finding itself in such a situation, may break a legal obligation to the extent necessary for the protection of its vital interests, although it must presumably do so without hurting vital interests of another country.[4]

When all else fails, states can invoke the clausula rebus sic stantibus. This clause entitles them to suspend or denounce a treaty if the circumstances prevailing at the conclusion of the treaty have very much changed against the state invoking the clause. As a tool for coping with social change, this clause caters to a real need (Kaplan and Katzenbach, 1961: 245). It can render service as a safety valve in an age of rapid social change (Schwarzenberger, 1967: 170). But the invention and use of this doctrine is another illustration of turning law into a handmaiden of politics. There is no objective way in the international system of determining when the conditions for the application of the clausula are fulfilled, making its invocation by a party to the treaty a political act. Moreover, by definition, the reasons for invoking the clausula are external to the law, possibly political, but in any case not legal (e.g., changes in the international power constellation, an improved bargaining position of one of the parties, basic alterations in national interests). Also, the conditions under which the clause may be invoked are not determinable by legal doctrine. They are located in the political arena, just as the reasons for concluding the treaty were located there. In other words, the clausula rebus sic stantibus is a legal cover for a political solution to a political problem.

In respect to this question of what is Caesar's and what is not, the Act of State Doctrine is at least frank, however controversial it otherwise is (see Bishop, 1971: 892, for literature). It too permits states an escape from international law for acts within the national territorial jurisdiction which are illegal internationally. For it states, as formulated by the United States Supreme Court, that "Every sovereign State is bound to respect the independence of every other sovereign State, and the courts of one country will not sit in judgment on the acts of the government of another done within its own territory" (Bishop, 1971: 881).

Legal Restraints Upon the Use of Power

The preference of many states for a regulated rather than an arbitrary use of power has led to the call for a separation of politics from law.[5] Proposals have been made that politics should be neutralized by the development of a comprehensive set of laws for all occasions (see Claude, 1962: 261-271). During the first year of the International Law Commission, Georges Scelle (United Nations, 1949: 38) defined the Commission's task as distinguishing what was legal even in the most political questions and as endeavoring "to enlarge the field of international law at the expense of that of politics." The Colombian delegate (United Nations, 1949: 38), agreeing with M. Scelle, suggested that the Commission "should avoid introducing politics into its work." In the course of time, many delegates to committees dealing with international law prided themselves in maintaining an "atmosphere of serenity" (e.g., United Nations, 1964d: 15; 1972: 305) as opposed, by implication, to the atmosphere of "dirty politics." Other delegates, however, presumably more aware of the different and necessary functions of both politics and law and of law's dependency upon politics, pointed out that the International Law Commission "was not a scientific body with purely academic terms of reference but a subsidiary organ of the General Assembly, itself a political body" (United Nations, 1949: 17, see also 21, 56; and 1947b: 9; 1967b: 5; 1963a: 53).

Legal restraints upon a state's use of its power potential are generated more by modern developments than by national wills. The existence of collective goods (biosphere) or undustributed goods (marine resources) necessitates an integrated approach for their handling. And integration could be the objective part of a community, favoring a more positive role of law. The increasing overlapping of interests among states causing more confrontations but also more cooperation (pluralism) again enhances the role of law while reducing the usefullness of arbitrary power application. A very similar effect is produced by the changing importance of the elements of power, with economic factors, prestige, and status matching that of physical force. There is, finally and still most importantly, the limit set to the arbitrary use of power by the existence of countervailing power. A balance of power toward which most states are striving makes states amenable to creating and obeying a legal regulation of given situations. Lassa Oppenheim (1912 I: 193) and other international lawyers (Geiger, 1964: 351, 353; Huber, 1910: 63; Scelle, 1932 I: 24; Stone, 1959: 39-40; Schwarzenberger, 1939: 75) argue that the balance of power was "an indispensable condition of the very existence of International Law," with Theodor Geiger expanding the argument to all kinds of law.

The balance of power as a main guarantor of international law fits into the diffusion of power in the international system. But the law so guaranteed shares the weaknesses of the balance of power. In particular, the reliance of law upon the balance of power for effectiveness could be self-defeating. With power unmeasurable, the balance becomes unmeasurable. The consequence of an unending competition for a power potential (e.g., the armaments race) often causes a neglect of the law in the name of the national interest. A paradox arises. Under the very favorable assumption that states aim at a balance of power as a sound foundation for international law, they are ignoring that law in the process of constructing such a foundation.

The scant success so far in harnessing the use of power to international law consistently is explained by the nature of power and its international organization. States can hardly be expected to provide for their existence under legal restraints whose enforcement is unreliable. Hitler (1938: 104) confirmed that when a state "is in danger of oppression or annihilation, the question of legality plays a subordinate role." Dean Acheson (1963: 13-14) stated more radically that "The survival of states is not a matter of law."

LIMITS TO LEGAL RESTRAINT ON POWER

Legal restraints upon the use of power are most difficult under the best of circumstances. The usefulness of everything to the power potential of states creates an almost impossible task for the lawmaker. He could not know what to regulate, or how. One and the same matter could serve a multitude of purposes. Regulating it for one purpose would then mean unwanted regulation also for other purposes. The problem is very acute in regard to the sources of nuclear energy, for instance, which states want to regulate when they are to be used for warlike purposes, but not for peaceful purposes. The complications get worse in regard to the imponderable elements of power. Is the stimulation of nationalism in many newer states a device for strengthening the country for future aggression or for turning it into a nation?

The problem was great during the nineteenth century when international lawyers held that disturbing the balance of power by one state might under certain conditions be illegal.[6] The definition of these conditions created the major problem, because nonmilitaristic internal improvements could at the same time objectively improve a nation's power potential. There was no way, for instance, of prohibiting a state's economic betterment because that would presumably also enhance its power potential.

Yet another reason for the inability of law to contain power effectively is that the struggle for power (and also the application of power) is cause and effect of international tensions. Tensions stem from historic memories about the behavior of states in general. Fear, distrust, suspicion, and hostility are some of its ingredients. They escape legal regulation. Not tension, but only some of its symptoms, especially concrete conflicts, can be handled by law. But the settlement of conflicts through legal measures, while helpful, could not settle the underlying tension. Tension could find expression in an unending number of conflicts, minor in themselves, but assuming important proportions as symptoms of the tension. An Israeli official stated convincingly (United Nations, 1969a: 296) that in the absence of a will for friendly relations and in the presence of grave tensions, the "operation of normal procedures" for the settlement of disputes was impaired. Legal processes "would at best superficially and formally solve certain technical problems without significantly contributing to the elimination of the real source of the dispute." One remedy would be the growth of a community in which fears, suspicions, and mistrust as the components of tension could be overcome, or where these factors could at least be balanced by common interests and loyalties to the group.

Fundamentally and ultimately, the absence of a community on the international scene is responsible for the role of power making the political system inadequate to perform its normal function of maintaining social order. It possesses the processes to be found in any political system: the use of power in arriving at social decisions, competition for power, and law-making and law-applying procedures for the control of social behavior. But the form of these processes and their institutionalization are so different that the political system has become unique and inadequate. Moreover, the weakness, for the same fundamental reason, of other social controls in the international society, places an intolerable burden upon the control function of international law.

NOTES

1. Territorial jurisdiction of the International Commission of the River Oder, Permanent Court of International Justice (1929: 26). See also Permanent Court of International Justice, Advisory Opinion No. 2 (1922) and No. 12 (1925) in Hudson (1934 I: 128, 737); Free Zones of Upper Savoy and the District of Gex, Permanent Court of International Justice (1932: 167); Wimbledon case, Permanent Court of International Justice (1923: 43); Kronprins Gustaf Adolf and Pacific cases in American Journal of International Law (1932: 882); Franco Italian Conciliation Commission and Egyptian Conseil d'Etat in Lauterpacht (annual, 1957: 481-482; annual, 1963: 291-292). But the European Court of Human Rights emphasized the need to realize the aim of a treaty before interpreting it in a manner "which would restrict to the greatest possible degree the obligations undertaken by the Parties" in the Wemhoff case in Lauterpacht (1970: 284). See also McDougal, Lasswell, and Miller (1967: 171-186) and Herczegh (1969: 72).

2. The reservation in the United States-Soviet Union Test Ban Treaty permitting each party to denounce the treaty is similarly worded. See p. 57.

3. On this topic, see Tucker (1966: 525-530). Judge Alvarez argued in the Ambatielos case that the International Court can deal with the judicial aspects of a dispute International Court of Justice (1952: 134).

4. Apparently the only case dealing with the "state of necessity" was the Neptune case in 1791 (Moore, 1931: 383-391). See also Cavaglieri (1929 I: 557-560), Verdross (1929 V: 488-490), Ago (1939 II: 540-545), Sørensen (1960 III: 219-221), von Liszt (1911: 182), and Carr (1949: 184-185).

5. Communist states are frank about the political nature of international law. In general, it is their theory, of course, that law is class law, hence political law. In specific instances they point this out expressly to weaken or reject rules they dislike. Starushenko (1969: 95) stated "International law is a sphere of relentless political struggle . . . ." At the Third Conference on the Law of the Sea at Caracas, the Chinese delegate stated that "The essence of the law of the sea was the struggle to defend sovereign security and natural resources of many medium-sized and small countries, and hence a serious political struggle" (United Nations, 1974d: 109).

6. For a discussion of the legal situation under the European balance of power system, see Westlake (1924: 332-333), Woolsey (1894: 45), and Davis (1908: 104-108).

Chapter 4

POLITICAL PROCESSES AND INTERNATIONAL LAW

The political processes and the law of the international society are determined by its management of power. The diffusion of power produces an identity of all political roles in states: they are political parties, legislators, executives, administrators, and, to a very large extent, judges. This undifferentiated role further enhances and interacts with the politicization of the entire society. It becomes nearly impossible to separate the various political, quasi-political, and nonpolitical functions in international relations. The political processes of the international society must therefore be defined broadly—more so than needs to be done for national societies. Any neat separation between, strictly speaking, political, legislative, administrative-executive, and judicial functions is quite unfeasible. When in the international society "politics" is to be studied, the legislative, administrative, and judicial processes must be included.

The Legislative Process

In the international society states want to do what normally government is doing for all the members of the national society.

They create most laws that bind them and execute them individually. At the San Francisco United Nations Conference on International Organization (vol. 13: 754; vol. 9: 70) a suggestion to grant the General Assembly legislative power was decisively rejected. Unless there is a rare coincidence of interests, hence consensus on a law, states struggle like other interest groups—though with different weapons—to make laws favoring their individual ends. The interests that eventually prevail and the law that secures them result from an adjustment of opposites in which each party obtains what it was powerful enough to obtain. Law, Arthur Bentley believed (1935: 273-274), is the "equilibration of interests, the balancing of groups." This is a benevolent opinion even for the best of states. In the international society, with its diffusion of power, law may still be a "balancing of groups." And the Iraqi delegate to the International Law Commission, Mr. Yasseen, asserted (United Nations, 1974a: 72) that the Commission "had always endeavoured to establish what represented the common interest or a balance of conflicting interests." But if so, the balancing is not necessarily on the basis of equilibrated interests. Instead, law all too often reflects the balance achieved in a trial of power in which states attempt to advance their individual interests, usually unmitigated by community considerations. To the extent that the power of each state produced laws favorable to itself, to that extent that state has been the maker of the law.

This character of the legislative process is very obvious in the case of treaty (conventional) law. Making treaties, especially multilateral treaties, is similar to the work of legislature. For although a treaty, like all other binding rules, is the outcome of a power contest between the signatories, all signatories can at least have the satisfaction of having participated in the process. Such participation, as Mr. Yasseen also pointed out, is a "guarantee of efficiency." It is simply slightly preferable to not having participated at all in the making of the law and yet be affected by it, as is often the case with customary law. Not only is the custom usually established by the more influential nations, customary law often only tells, as an Indian and Algerian official expressed it (United Nations, 1968: 3; 1966d: 11), what the law "had been rather than what it actually is," and how it had been made "in other times by a small international community." As far as the newer states are concerned, recognition of a customary rule of law is most often a law-confirming rather than a law-creating process, although it remains even then a political process.

There are two differences worth pointing out in the international legislative process as compared to national processes. One, not too important, relates to the target of the law. In national societies, the objects of the law are always categories of citizens: all drivers must carry licenses. Bills of attainder or laws ad personam are very rare. In the international society only signatories are bound by their treaties and even customary law need not bind states making clear that they do not subscribe to the custom. But this is not sufficiently satisfactory to many states because it is one thing not to be bound by a law and quite another not to be affected by that law. In this age of interaction what affects any two states very often affects many other states. For this reason, especially, smaller and newer states are claiming a right to participate in the making of multilateral treaties dealing with matters of concern to states other than the signatories. At the Vienna Conference of 1968-1969 on the Law of Treaties, a clause was introduced, but not accepted, that "Every State has a right to participate in a multilateral treaty which codifies or progressively develops norms of general international law or the object and purpose of which are of interest to the international community of States as a whole" (United Nations, 1969a: 181). In preparation of the Third Conference of the Law of the Sea, the Soviet delegate, favoring the principle of consensus instead of majority rule in certain situations, argued (Sohn, 1975: 333) that the only method of solving questions relating to the creation of new law was consensus. "We are firmly convinced that it is only on the basis of this principle—on the basis of a sensible harmonization of the principles of justice and taking into account the interest of all States—that we can create norms of international law which will be observed and can ensure that the conventions which finally emerge will be ratified by a sufficiently large number of States" (United Nations, 1973a: 21-22). The Chinese delegate, however, branded the "imposition" of the principle of consensus as "tantamount to a veto" and "typical hegemonism" (United Nations, 1973b: 22-23).

This pressure for an international legislative process has as a correlate the refusal by many newer states to succeed into even multilateral treaties of a universal character without their express approval. They favor the "clean slate" principle over the "opting out" principle, by which is meant that successor states are not bound by any treaties to which they have not specifically and positively agreed after obtaining independence (instead of being automatically bound by treaties concluded by their predecessor states until they have given notice of termination [United Nations, 1974a: 247; 1974b: 1308-1393]). They are insisting on the well-known principle that universal rules of international law should be created only by universal agreement of all states.

The other difference distinguishing national from international law-making as a political process is crucial. It relates to the role power is allowed to play. In national legislative processes (and somewhat depending upon the particular political system) power cannot be used in an arbitrary fashion and its use is restricted to certain means and methods (thus, e.g., agreement cannot be reached by the threat of violence and the use of force is not available to the parties).

This management of power still permits the powerful to triumph, mainly because they presumably created and maintain the conditions under which the legislative process takes place. But they triumph without threatening the social order because all parties concerned more or less acquiesce in the conditions. They do so, most frequently, because all citizens, powerful and powerless, share a loyalty to the national community. The law guaranteeing these conditions of the legislative process is obeyed and enforced, preventing arbitrary power and safeguarding orderly functioning. It commands allegiance, as Harold Laski put it (1931: 39), when it "strikes such a balance of interests that what emerges as satisfied is greater than can be secured by any alternative programme."

As long as such a balance of interests can be established states will create and support law. But such a balance is always labile, not only because of the absence of an enduring common interest among states but also because states tend very readily to endow their own individual interests with a vital quality. Then, when interests clash, states often consider their very existence at stake and for such moments they developed their power potential and retained their discretion of using it. Power, not law, becomes the ultimate tool for the execution of foreign policy. The paradox is that in contrast to national societies where the force of the law becomes strongest when the survival of the citizen is threatened, international law and the legislative process become weakest when they are needed most to safeguard the social order. In times of crisis states choose to deal with each other mainly on political terms. Their relations become a pure contest of power, in which law goes by the board and the legislative process is transmuted into a match of national strengths.

An "alternative programme" to the chaos following the arbitrary use of power is perceivable. When the alternative program to a balancing of interests becomes the dropping of atom bombs, states can become quite ingenious in building a balance. They are assisted by the growth in kinds and volume of their international interests. Both developments provide more opportunities for bargaining toward establishing a balance and for making it more enduring by the possibilities of overlapping and substituting these interests. The area of reciprocity among states is widening, and reciprocity is fertile grounds for effective law.

The evidence of this development can readily be found in the increasing number of treaties, especially multilateral and so-called political treaties. Even when states are not parties they are "bound" by these treaties in the sense that the conditions created for the nonparticipating states are just as real as for the signatories. Every state had to adjust, for instance, to the international order created by the treaties of Vienna in 1814-1815, Versailles in 1914, and San Francisco in 1945. Exactly because of these consequences so many states argued at the Vienna conference that they should all have a right to participate in certain multilateral treaties, otherwise their sovereignty would be useless. The International Court of Justice advised in the Reparations for Injuries case (1949: 179) that the states creating the United Nations, "representing the vast majority of the members of the international community," had the power in conformity with international law to bring into being the United Nations possessing "objective international personality" which all states, nonmember states as well, had to recognize with all the consequences such recognition implied.

There exists a trend toward more international legislation, although an international legislature is a very remote possibility (see Jenks, 1969: 166-169). "Power politics" continues to dominate the international scene. But its hegemony is weakening as force is being supplemented by economic, social, and cultural factors as elements of the power potential. The chance of creating and maintaining a more reliable balance is improving as a result. These elements of the power potential could also be used unilaterally as weapons. Economic warfare is a common occurrence in international politics. But its conduct is increasingly difficult as the division of labor spreads across the globe and mutual sensitivities among states grow. This process conduces to the strengthening of the legislative process (i.e., mainly treaty-making). Power retains an important role and always will, but it is increasingly power tamed by mutual interests.

The Judicial Process

The prospect for adequate judicial processes is not as favorable. There is greater pressure for the legal regulation of state behavior than for judicial interpretation of the law or the judicial settlement of international disputes. States are hesitant to bind themselves to law, but they are even more hesitant to be bound to it by a court. The rationale for this attitude was provided by an official from Sierra Leone (United Nations, 1968: 407) when he stated that "no judgment could be delivered impartially or without intervention of political or extra-juridical consideration." Experience with the methods for the peaceful settlement of disputes shows that their use decreases as the participation of third parties increases.

It may seem paradoxical that nevertheless the International Court of Justice, like its predecessor, the Permanent Court of International Justice, is formally the best developed international political institution and probably the most respected in the abstract. One solution of the paradox is that the Court was created, in part, as an appeasement of those who demanded it as a war aim. But its roots go deeper, reaching back to the turn of the century when the Permanent Court of Arbitration was created at the first Hague Conference (1899) and thereafter improved at the second Hague Conference (1907). The time "seemed ripe" for these Courts, to quote Manley O. Hudson (1938: 1-2), and the birth of the Permanent Court of International Justice was then "taken for granted." Their formal perfection could perhaps be agreed upon because there also was a widespread assumption that their role would be minor. It is also a historical experience that the formalization of a judiciary precedes that of a legislature or administration. The reason may be that it is more difficult to agree upon what the law shall be than upon its interpretation and application. The judicial function quite erroneously is assumed to be "nonpolitical" because it merely follows the making of social decisions and of the law. Those subjecting themselves to the judicial process can then feel that they are running low risks because the outcome is within the range of previous agreement upon the law. States favoring compulsory adjudication of international disputes have therefore argued that no restriction of sovereignty is involved because any limitation of freedom occurred when a treaty or other agreement was concluded "rather than at the stage of arbitral or judicial procedure, which was merely the consequence and complement of conclusion" (United Nations, 1969a: 277, also 292, 294).

This conception of the judicial, as distinguished from the political, led to the demand for a separation of the International Court from politics. A distinction was therefore made–and acknowledged by the Court–between legal and political or justiciable and nonjusticiable disputes (see Lauterpacht, 1933: 153-165; Tucker, 1966: 525-530; Stone, 1959: 146-152; Bloomfield, 1958). In the first category were disputes caused by disagreement between the parties concerning their rights and obligations, and these could be handled by the Court. The subject matter of the second category was more uncertain, to the point where no adequate definition has yet been found. Judge Kellogg defined it as everything "exclusively within the competence of a sovereign State," such as immigration, tariff rates, and taxation (in the case of the Free Zones . . ., 1930: 41-42). An Austrian official (United Nations, 1969a: 285) defined it as "relating to vital interests, frontier delimitations and so forth." A Swiss official, with the agreement of colleagues from many other countries (United Nations, 1969a: 269, also 278, 279, 286; and 1969b: 246), suggested ignoring the question because the two types of disputes always involved a subjective element and no objective distinction was possible.

The point the Swiss official was making was, of course, exactly the reason why states, in practice, continue to make the distinction.

It enables them to escape from any obligation to submit their disputes to judicial settlement, either as a general obligation or as a treaty commitment. Already at the first Hague Conference the Russian delegate expressed a national position which has remained typical when he said that no government "would consent *in advance* to assume the obligation to submit to the decision of an arbitral tribunal every dispute which might arise in the international domain if it concerned the national honor of a State, or its highest interests, or its inalienable possessions" (Proceedings of the Hague Conferences, 1920: 173-174; see also United Nations, 1969a: 289, 293, 301). The reluctance of states to have their disputes adjudicated finds expression, first, in limiting their obligation of submitting to judicial procedures, and second, in limiting the jurisdiction of the Court when they do submit to judicial procedures.

States have consistently rejected the notion of a general and universal obligation of submitting all their disputes to an international court. They have almost as adamantly opposed voluntary agreements to submit their disputes to judicial decisions by international courts (the so-called "compulsory jurisdiction"). This was true, for example, in the case of arbitration in general, of the two international courts, of the Law of the Sea Conference (1958), the Conference on Diplomatic Intercourse and Immunities (1961), the Conference on Consular Relations (1963), the Conference on the Law of Treaties (1968-1969), the Third Law of the Sea Conference (1975).[1] Whenever "compulsory" jurisdiction was proposed, it was rejected in favor of "optional procedures" by which states had the option of choosing which method for peaceful settlement or disputes they wanted to apply. The nearest to an obligation for judicial settlement is the "optional clause" in Article 36 of the Statute of the International Court of Justice and certain commitments of Western European states to the use of the European Court of Justice.

Under this very limited obligation, states then define narrowly the competence of the court, mainly by defining what questions the court is entitled to decide and on the basis of what principles or rules. In the first place the whole group of "political" disputes is excluded. The International Court in the case of the Customs Régime between Germany and Austria (1931: 75, see also 68) and in other cases subsequently asserted that "The Court is not concerned with political considerations nor with political consequences. These lie outside its competence."[2] But disagreement among the judges themselves demonstrated how difficult it is to make distinctions. There would be no difficulty in showing the political character of some of the Court's decisions. In the second place, Article 36 of the Court's Statute enumerates the legal questions states are willing to let the Court decide. In the third place, the Court is instructed either by Statute or by agreement among the parties what law is to be applied. In the fourth place, states may accept the optional clause of Article 36 in the Court's Statute with reservations—leading to the notorious Connally Amendment (see p. 55) making the entire acceptance of the "compulsory jurisdiction" meaningless and invalid, in the opinion of Judge Lauterpacht. Moreover, the International Court of Justice decided on several occasions that the principle of reciprocity permits states not having Connally-type reservations to invoke them nevertheless against states having them, thus extending the effective range of the reservation.

All states, large and small, rich and poor, strong and weak, prefer the option of settling disputes by their own means. During the conference on the Law of Treaties, many smaller or weaker states acknowledged their dilemma. A Bolivian admitted that treaties and their adjudication were "the only recourse open to weak countries in their relations with other countries." An Ivory Coastan assured his colleagues that "the introduction of compulsory jurisdiction could not conflict with the interests of the newly independent countries, which were unable to fall back on force." In the words of a Pakistani, the absence of compulsory jurisdiction of a court when two states failed to agree "would mean a unilateral decision by the more powerful" (United Nations, 1969a: 282, 278, 276, see also 277, 275).

Most states find the reasons against compulsory jurisdiction of international courts more convincing. Law is imprecise, incomplete, and inadequate, many argue. The outcome of a judgment can be highly uncertain. The International Court is conservative and may use outmoded law for its decisions—another argument. The newer states often claim that the judges do not represent their culture area and can use customary and other legal rules to which they have not contributed. It may even happen, they fear, that laws or treaties from the colonial era may still be found valid.[3] In the light of all these possibilities, the Secretary General of the United Nations found it "understandable" (United Nations, 1955a: xiii) that states have a tendency to seek a political settlement of their disputes even in cases where a question of law lies at the heart of the dispute.

The cogency of these arguments is weakening. The law the International Court applies rests increasingly on multilateral treaties in which more and more of the newer states participate. The law is thereby adapted to contemporary requirements and responsive to the needs of newer states. Moreover, there have always been judges willing to move with the times and to interpret international law in accordance with modern conditions. The Court can stimulate the development of progressive law. To the very limited extent that it does, the power factor in the creation of law diminishes. The Court, for obvious reasons, is hesitant to admit that it is creating new law. It has repeatedly affirmed that it is "to interpret the treaties, not to revise them" (Interpretation of Peace Treaties case, 1950: 229). But the fact alone that there are disputes over the meaning of the law indicates that the Court decides what it is. Interpretation becomes a legislative, hence to some extent a political act. Some of the Court's judges have freely admitted this activity. "It cannot be denied" said Judge Ammoun in the North Sea Continental Shelf case (1969: 136) "that an international court, by progressively diverging from the thesis of the formal or logical plenitude of international law, contributes to the remedying of its insufficiencies and the filling-in of its lacunae."[4]

This possibility is exactly what discourages some states from using the Court in their disputes.[5] Their arguments are that they do not know what law the Court will create, and that in creating law the Court will be subject to powerful pressures. Cuba expressed this suspicion most forcefully when its spokesman stated (United Nations, 1969a: 301): "In certain matters international law was no more than the adaptation of foreign policy to the needs of the moment. In an atmosphere where power prevailed over justice, it can not reasonably be expected that the decisions of a body consisting of third parties would be fair and effective."

The wish of states to reserve as large an area of uninhibited action as possible applies to the judicial process as well. To them, the judicial process is acceptable only under rare circumstances. For either they fear that the process is itself political, or they hope they can achieve more favorable results by using political means for the solution of their disputes. Either case is another illustration of the politicization of the international society. The observance of international law, the use that is made of it, and when and how judicial means are being adopted remain political decisions (see Henkin, 1965 I: 189-191). And this also applies to the use of the International Court (Rosenne, 1961: 56-62; 1973: 162-167).

The Administrative Process

The administrative process shares with the judicial process a widespread reputation of being nonpolitical. The political process is assumed to have ended with the making of the law which thereafter the judge and administrator are expected to carry out and apply. The administrator in the presumably postpolitical phase is to translate laws and policies into behavior. The expectation has been that international administration would present few problems to international cooperation. Indeed, the dissection of international relations into specific functions and the granting of authority to specific agencies to handle such functions were not so long ago believed to be the surest path to "one world." It was believed that politics and the political separation of states would succumb to demands for international services which no governments would or could deny. Recent development bore out to some extent this belief, but not yet sufficiently to affect the basic nature of international politics and law.

The distinction between the making and the executing of the law is obscured by a very broad borderline in which both overlap under the best of circumstances. In international politics, the distinction is virtually nonexistent. One reason is that, similar to the judge's task, the administrator's is to implement the law by defining what specific behavior or action is required. This is a continuation of the legislative process and the administrator's decision is, in fact, political (see Fried, 1971: 156; Waldock, 1963: 367; Stone, 1959: 138). The second reason is the politicization of the international society, which affects administration as much as anything else. As Georg Schwarzenberger pointed out (1967: 261), the essence of administration is freedom of action and the exercise of discretion within the constitutional limits of the administrative agency. But giving an international agency such freedom and discretion is, in principle, anathema to sovereign states. Their political considerations wipe out the distinction between administrative and political activity (Yemin, 1969: 19). Only most hesitantly and in response to almost irresistible need are they willing to grant an international administrator freedom of action in usually very technical (i.e., nonpolitical) matters.

For this reason, administrative international agencies are of very recent date, and those that exist are normally very limited in their powers. Only during the last hundred years or so did such agencies develop from fewer than ten to many hundreds, and clearly as a reaction to technical developments, accompanied by growing demands for governmental services. These agencies were initially called international public or international administrative unions, mainly to emphasize their nonpolitical, and narrow, technical functions. But as the number and nature of these function broadened, and especially as these functions became an integral part of a state's political existence, the borderline between administration, politics, and law could no longer be drawn with any accuracy. International safety arrangements for shipping on the Danube could conceivably be purified from politics for awhile, but could the international policing of a truce line between Israel and Egypt ever be? Moreover, the newer agencies were performing mixed functions, with a comprehensive multipurpose agency such as the United Nations performing potentially every kind of function. As a result the concept of a separate international administrative function and international administrative law went out of fashion. The broader concept of international organization was substituted in which, to a large extent, political, legal, judicial, and administrative activities were synthesized.

International Law and International Organization

From the standpoint of international law, treaties creating international organizations are useful because their contribution to law is not generally exhausted with their conclusion. Creation of the organization is not the final stage of such a contribution. The organization is likely to be an active, operational institution. It leads to further agreements and treaties in pursuit of its purpose, which moreover may have near-universal qualities if the organization has globally or regionally a large membership and a multiplicity of functions. But just because of this characteristic, states are extremely cautious in giving organizations inherent power to bind them. Because in most cases the treaty constituting the organization is not self-executing, politics continues beyond its conclusion. Although the activities of the organization are defined and limited by its constitution, they require continuing political agreement among the members. The more comprehensive the scope of the organization, the more politics takes place within it, and states wish to retain continuous control over it. Here lies the basic reason for the denial of legislative capacity to international organizations.

The United Nations illustrates well this situation. It is far removed from the ideal picture of a supranational body creating international rules and regulations of a universal nature. It is, in fact, nearer to being a political tool. Much of the practice in the United Nations has been to embarrass opponents, to sharpen hostilities, and to create excuses for the escalation of conflicts. Friendly nations do not bring their disputes to the United Nations. When hostile nations do so, they consider it almost an unfriendly act. Under such conditions states usually refuse to accept conclusions as binding. They consider them political pronouncements, and most often rightly so (see Yeselson and Gaglione, 1974).

This description applies particularly to the General Assembly and the Security Council, but holds true for other organs as well. A study of eight specialized agencies (Cox and Jacobson, 1973: 389) concluded that "the greater the immediate practical consequences are in material terms, the more the predominant influence is likely to be exercised by the governments." The same conclusion can be drawn for all other international organizations—even for the European Coal and Steel Community notwithstanding its supranational features. The broad principles and the generous promises for their implementation to be found in the preambles of constitutions of international organizations are usually in stark contrast to the narrowly and carefully circumscribed commitments entered into by member states. These, not the high-sounding preambulary tenets, represent the "unnecessarily timid least-common denominator," because states are rarely willing to commit resources, political will, or sovereignty for the noble objectives and great visions enshrined in the preambles of the constitutions of international organizations (Hargrove, 1972: 41-42).

But because no constitution can foresee all eventualities, states are unable to specify the limits of their obligation with precision. While their inclination obviously is to err on the side of giving an organization too little jurisdiction and authority, they also want the organization to function, which may require some scope for autonomous action. The general solution to this problem has been to assume that an organization has the right to do what is necessary for fulfilling its function. In rare cases, this doctrine of implied powers has been embodied in constitutions (e.g., Article 95 of the European Coal and Steel Community; Article 6 of the Council for Mutual Economic Assistance). More often it remains unexpressed in documents. When the United Nations was established, for instance, it was stated (United Nations Conference on International Organization, 1945: 70) that "in the course of the operations from day to day of the various organs of the Organization, it is inevitable that each organ will interpret such parts of the Charter as are applicable to its particular functions. This process is inherent in the functioning of any body which operates under an instrument defining its functions." The International Court of Justice in the Reparations for Injuries case (1949: 182) confirmed that under international law the United Nations "must be deemed to have the powers, which, though not expressly provided by the Charter, are conferred upon it by necessary implication as being essential to the performance of its duties." In the Effects of Awards of Compensation case (1954: 57) the Court stated again that the capacity of the United Nations to create an Administrative Tribunal for the decision of internal disputes arose from "necessary intendment out of the Charter" (for details on the doctrine, see Detter, 1965: 29-34; Seidl-Hohenveldern, 1967: 202-203; Schneider, 1963: 138). In the majority of the cases, the powers that are deemed implied relate to internal affairs of organizations. Occasionally they comprise the making of treaties with the host country, or with countries receiving aid and assistance from the organization. But no matter how far one wishes to stretch the doctrine of implied powers, the law-making capacity of organizations is small. Nothing more comprehensive was to be expected from sovereign states in regard to the broad-minded doctrine of implied powers. On the contrary, they have normally explicitly rejected any idea that acts of an international organization might be "legislative" and could bind member states.

This question is controversial mainly among writers of international law.[6] In the practice of states final acts or general pronouncements of international organizations are usually denied any legally binding force, no matter whether they were called declarations, resolutions, recommendations, decisions, conclusions, suggestions, instructions, directions, appeals, authorizations, adoptions, or whatever. The Repertory of United Nations Practice (1955b: 569) stated that the term decision in regard to the General Assembly "is used in a broad sense to cover all types of actions by United Nations organs," Including recommendations (which would inherently not bind states). On innumerable occasions and in many different international agencies states have asserted, without contradiction, that final acts have no legally binding force.[7] There are exceptions. The United States maintained that the United Nations resolution on the Peaceful Uses of Outer Space "constituted international law." But France, with the agreement of the Soviet Union and other states, immediately contradicted the United States, arguing that United Nations resolutions were merely "declarations of intent" and could not give rise to legal obligations unless they were incorporated in subsequent international agreements (United Nations, 1966n: 5, 9, 10, 15; 1966o: 5; 1966p: 2, 3; 1966q: 6).

In view of this extremely limited legislative power of international organizations, their benefits for international law must be sought in more indirect contributions. They might be said to have what Georges Scelle (in a different context) called (United Nations, 1949: 21) "pre-legislative" power. They do preparatory and preliminary work on new law. They are stimulants for the regulation of new international functions through legal norms. They have research and drafting facilities. Their actions can clarify legal problems. They can refine legal concepts; develop customs; uncover legal principles. The organizations are not international legislatures. Their competence for creating international law is minimal (see Tunkin, 1974: 242).

The hope of some smaller and weaker states that their participation in international organizations would enable them to share in international law-making was futile. Even the expectation that under the principle of sovereign equality their equality is better preserved in organizations than in bilateral relations remained unfulfilled, for the reason that politics continues into the administration of charters and constitutions. One very obvious indicator of such politics, making for considerable inequality of states, is the favored position often granted to the most powerful states in the form of veto rights, weighted voting, or guaranteed seats in commissions and committees, usually in bodies where final acts may indeed have some obligating character (which excludes, for instance, the General Assembly; see Schwarzenberger, 1967: 265). To speak of international organizations, and even of the administrative processes within them, as "quasi-legislative" is nurturing a comforting illusion. International organizations are an extension and remain under the control of individual states.[8] Power, a crucial factor in law-making, rests with the member states. They have in exceptional cases delegated some of their power or lent their sovereignty to international agencies—but almost always with the possibility of recall. International organizations fail thereby to be either substitutes for states or independent subjects of international law. As administrative or executive agencies they are dependencies, not equals, of states (see Lukashuk, 1969: 179-187).

Legal Limits on Politics

The examination of the major political processes in their relation to law reveals the continuous pressure from states to have politics prevail over law. On the grounds that the weakest link determines the strength of the chain, the effect of law remains weak even in regard to less than vital interests of states because they insist upon preserving a legal system giving them maximum freedom of action when vital interests are at stake. If further proof is needed, it can be found in the refusal of the Security Council (with the exceptions of the Corfu Channel and Namibia cases) to refer cases for decision or opinion to the International Court of

Justice—in spite of Article 36 of the Charter inviting it to do so. The Security Council does not disregard the law. On the contrary, much of the language used is legal. But the procedure employed is nonjudicial and decisions are reached through parliamentary methods. Law serves, essentially, as a means of communication—still a useful, but not an ideal, purpose (see Kahng, 1964: 227-236; Alexy, 1961).

That the potentially most powerful states should take this approach to politics and law is understandable. But smaller, weaker, and newer states are not entirely averse to it. They too cherish freedom of action and build up their power potential in support of it. But in view of the enormous differences in the power potentials, they are attempting to use legal restraints upon politics to create greater political equality. Their way of doing this is to make the exerting of pressure by one state against another illegal. If they were to succeed, it would mean the neutralization of power and the abolition of politics altogether. For one state influencing through pressure another state to produce a desired behavior is the application of power, and this, in turn, is the essence of politics.

The attempt is not new. Force and coercion as means of pressure have long been condemned. Under the Charter and other international instruments they have become illegal. In regard to other means of pressure, the legal situation is less clear. For instance, the support of revolutionaries, the intervention in civil wars, and the quarantine of states have a dubious legal nature. "Indirect" aggression through subversion and propaganda has not yet been regulated internationally. There is even less international agreement on means such as "economic aggression" or "cultural imperialism." With the growing international interaction, even the exploitation of ordinary bargaining positions, considered normal in times past, might be defined as undue pressure, especially between unequal partners. The Chinese, for instance, for over a hundred years have tried to obtain political concessions from foreign states in return for an opportunity to trade in a market of hundreds of millions of customers. Under contemporary conditions, such means assume greater prominence as elements of power and those involving force become less applicable so that the meaning of "pressure" is subject to change.

Many states are therefore insisting now that the concepts of "force" and "coercion" must be expanded to include all forms of political and economic pressure. An early reference to this idea can be found in a project of the International Commission of American Jurists which stated in 1927 that states are equal before the law and that "the rights of each are dependent not upon the power which it possesses to ensure the exercise of them but solely upon the fact of their existence as a person of international law." This formulation was adopted thereafter in several inter-American conventions (see United Nations, 1948: 66-67). The expanded version appeared in the Charter of the Organization of American States in 1948, which defines intervention in Article 15 as "any form of interference or attempted threat against the personality of the state or against its political, economic and cultural elements." Article 16 of the Charter declares illegal "the use of coercive measures of an economic or political character in order to force the sovereign will of another State and obtain from it advantages of any kind." The nonaligned states at the Belgrade (1961) and Cairo (1964) meetings adopted resulutions prohibiting the use of political or economic pressures among states. In 1965 the General Assembly of the United Nations adopted a resolution favoring the elimination of such pressures (see United Nations, 1968: 270).

This broadening of the concept force was frequently discussed in international conferences (see Arangio-Ruiz, 1972 III: 528-530). A number of arguments were produced in favor of including nonviolent or nonphysical means (United Nations, 1966r: 11; 1966k: 12, 14; 1966l: 22; 1968: 273, 274, 276; Asian African Legal Consultative Committee, 1967: 46). Ignoring this new means of pressure would make a farce of freedom of decision and consent among states. The new pressure was the essence of neo-colonialism and intended to achieve the ends formerly accomplished with conquest and occupation. Force had to be interpreted dynamically; the United Nations Charter was not an historic document but a living document. At the time of its signing force may have been essentially physical force. Today, economic force was the real force and with its aid, states could be effectively controlled and their sovereignty turned into an empty formula.

One qualification those states favoring the expanded concept were willing to grant. All pressures should be prohibited only if they would have "the effect of threatening the territorial integrity or political independence of any State" (United Nations, 1966s: 1; similarly 1966t: 2; 1966u: 2; see also Falk, 1966 I: 44-63).

The opposing states, a minority, argued that force as used in the Charter meant physical force only. They argued that there was not yet an adequate definition of political and economic pressure to make binding legal agreements concerning them. While some forms of pressure should certainly be condemned, it was quite another thing and a threat to international stability to declare agreements and actions null, void, or illegal on the allegation that pressure had been used. Great Britain elaborated on the absurd consequences which could follow from making such vague concepts part of legal instruments. For instance, when a state refused to sell something another state wanted to buy, the refusal could become an illegal act of aggression. The United States maintained that no useful purpose could be served by turning legal instruments "into a more or less indiscriminate catalogue of legal, moral and political wrongs" (United Nations, 1966k: 15-16; 1966l: 6, 7, 8, 13; 1968: 272, 275, 291, 292; 1952: 58; 1964d: 13).

The Secretary General in his Annual Report for 1952 (United Nations, 1952: 58) sided with the minority view when he stated that "the concept of economic aggression appears particularly liable to extend the concept of aggression almost indefinitely. The acts in question not only do not involve the use of force, but are usually carried out by a State by virtue of its sovereignty or discretionary power. Where there are no commitments a State is free to fix its customs tariffs and to limit or prohibit exports and imports. If it concludes a commercial treaty with another State, superior political, economic and financial strength may of course give it an advantage over the weaker party; but that applies to every treaty, and it is difficult to see how such inequalities, which arise from differences in situation, can be evened out short of changing the entire structure of international society and transferring powers inherent in States to international organs."

Even such a change would not guarantee substantive equality. There is no political system that could eliminate differences between the members of the society or their consequences in practice. In particular, as D. P. O'Connell (1965: vol. 1, 325) pointed out, "A general condemnation of 'economic aggression' is about as intellectually valuable a conception as is 'imperialism' in contemporary political jargon." Later he added that there was an "inherent impossibility of comprehending in the one juridicial category every conceivable form of economic and social domination of States by one another." (In December 1974, the General Assembly resolved to define aggression as "the use of armed force.")

The usefulness of expanding the concept of force to include political and economic pressure in general lies in drawing attention to an existing problem. Its solution is hardly possible by abolishing it legally. A solution is more likely to come—as indeed it is coming—through agreements settling specific and identifiable grievances, such as those relating to terms of trade, import and export quotas, tariffs, and dumping in the economic sphere; or as those in the political sphere such as radio propaganda, foreign bases, and alliance manipulations. Such a solution appeals to the preference of states for well-defined, limited obligations and is based more on reciprocity, which remains a favorable foundation for effective law.

The conception of power as these newer and smaller states are using it involves coercion under contemporary (and past) conditions. What they are apparently aiming at is to limit power in the international sphere to what Klaus Knorr calls "nonpower influence" (1975: 310-319). By this is meant the ability by one society "to affect the behavior of another society without any adversary resort to superior strength, military or economic." Where such a situation prevails, it is beneficial because it enriches the choices of all concerned. To some extent, such a conceptualization of power or nonpower is a matter of semantics. Contrary to the way power is used here, namely, as any kind of influence however produced, only coercive influence or the unilateral creation of a fait accompli is defined as power. To some extent also such nonpower influence relationships between states obtain in considerable volume when a balance of interests exists between them (see p. 66). But even then politics remains prevalent. More important, because unbalanced relationships in international relations are so frequent and their results can be vital to states, their consequences for the nature of international politics and the role of power crucially determine the nature of the entire international system and the role of power in it.

Attempts in the international society to confine the practice of politics within a set of regulations is always incongruous, although some in fact have been successful. But it is one thing to make legal rules for the game of politics. It is quite another to legislate politics out of existence. To ban all forms of political and economic pressure from international relations is tantamount to banishing reality.

NOTES

1. For some details on these conferences, see United Nations (1969a: 266; 1966m: 24-29; 1975); see also Jenks (1964: 13-118).

2. See also International Court of Justice, Ambatielos case (1952: 134), North Sea Continental Shelf (1969: 166), Permanent Court of International Justice, Free Zones of Upper Savoy and the District of Gex, series A (1930: 29-43), and Green (1970: 669).

3. For examples, see United Nations (1969a: 241, 274, 282, 291; 1964e: 6; 1966a: 11; 1964b: 94-95). See also Shepherd (1969: 114-142), Anand (1969: 54-72), and Schröder (1970: 41-44).

4. See also International Court of Justice, Anglo-Norwegian Fisheries case (1951: 146), United Nations (1966a: 7), Anand (1969: 152-190), and Lauterpacht (1934).

5. The Soviet Union approves of the International Court in principle, but is very critical of several of its judgments and of the use some states have made of it (Academy of Sciences of the USSR, n.d.: 396). The People's Republic of China is, in principle, opposed to the International Court, but has not hesitated on occasion to refer to its decisions when they were useful in justifying some Chinese action (Kaminski, 1973: 219-223; Hsiung, 1972: 309-314; Leng and Chiu, 1972: 100).

6. Schwelb (1966), Yemin (1969: 206-214), Detter (1965: 319-329), Jenks (1969: 186-200), Castañeda (1970 I), Pallieri (1969 II), Arangio-Ruiz (1972 III: 431-518–providing a comprehensive survey). See also International Court of Justice, South-West Africa case (1966: 441), Tammes (1958 II), and Tunkin (1974: 171).

7. For examples, see United Nations (1961d: 133; 1947c: 10; 1960a: 270, 273; 1960b: 1415, 1420, 1427; Repertory of the United Nations, 1955b: 269).

8. The major exception is in the law of the European Economic Community. Community treaties provide that the decisions or resolutions of certain executive agencies of the organization become automatically binding as internal law of the member states (see Waldock, 1962 II: 132-133; Teitgen, 1971 III; Kapteyn and van Themaat, 1973: 25-31).

Chapter 5

THE SOURCES OF INTERNATIONAL LAW

The answer to where international law originates depends upon the intent of the question. It could be directed at the ultimate roots of the law and thus be philosophically oriented. It could also be highly pragmatically oriented and direct itself simply to the places where the law may be found. And it could also refer to other origins between these extremes. (See the discussion by Tucker, 1966: 437-440; Herczegh, 1969: 57-68; Parry, 1965: 1-27.)

For the purposes of the International Court of Justice the various sources where the judges are to find the law are enumerated in Article 38 of the Statute: international conventions, international custom, general principles of law, and, within limits, judicial decisions and the teachings of the most highly qualified publicists. The law expressed in these sources is traditionally divided into several categories, among them general and particular, customary general and particular, codified, conventional (treaty), and principles and norms.

Earlier it has been mentioned that the entire culture of a society could be the source of law. The social facts are its raw material. All those can be the makers of the law who actively, and even passively, participate in the process eventuating in specific legislation. Numberless institutions contribute to the creation of the law.

Such a comprehensive approach to the "legislative" process pays its respect to the unity of social existence, where everything is related to everything else, and where, more specifically (generalizing a proposal by an American delegate to the United Nations [United Nations, 1963b: 7]), social problems must be solved "in terms which are legally sound and politically viable." The "policy-oriented" approach to international law is founded on this broad perspective (McDougal, Lasswell, and others). So is the Communists' approach, for the quite different purpose of rationalizing their selective acceptance of legal obligations. In the words of a Chinese writer (Leng and Chiu, 1972: 10) "the substantive sources of bourgeois international law are the external policy of the bourgeoisie which is also the will of the ruling class of those big capitalist powers." Soviet international lawyers take the similar position that "International Law, like any other law, pertains to the superstructure and is of a class character" (Academy of Sciences of the USSR, n.d.: 10; see also Herczegh, 1969: 57-59). These Communist states can thus combine recognition of international law in general with disobedience to specific rules they consider class-bound.

Four dissenting judges of the International Court in the case Reservations on the Convention on Genocide (1951: 46; see also Schachter, 1971: 9-15) appeared ready to adopt a broad perspective when they suggested a restriction on sovereignty in favor of a more policy-oriented function of international law. They said: "It is undeniable that the tendency of all international activities in recent times has been toward the promotion of the common welfare of the international community . . . ." Consequently, they proposed that this tendency must be considered in all legal matters.

But the dilemma is that such a comprehensive approach complicates the analysis of the sources of international law, as of all particular aspects of the international society. The complexities of the international, as of any, society are such that all parts of its totality cannot always be equally considered in the investigation of any one of its parts. While it is inevitable that the sources—material or formal—of international law are related to all aspects of that society, some limits upon the consideration of other aspects are imperative if the study of the sources is to be productive. They must be relegated to serve as the background or the context. An incidental advantage of doing this is that the focus on the forms "in which the rules of international law are expressed and laid down" (G. I. Tunkin) as they exist within the political framework of the international society facilitates a common enterprise by those who otherwise take different perspectives on the origins of international law. Although "source" will here be used in this narrower sense, it is not thereby considered purified of its political derivation.

The Multiplicity of Sources

The decentralization of the international political system and its extreme politicization are responsible for such a scattering, uncoordination, and vagueness of the sources of law as well as for their multiplicity that even law-abiding states can have legitimate disputes over the fact or nature of their obligations. Very often, the law is not readily found. Disagreements are frequent regarding what law should be applied before there is agreement that the law should be applied. There can be unending debate over the nature of general principles of law recognized by civilized states or over custom engaged in by states in their belief that to do so is obligatory. There is a relative scarcity of universal rules in the absence of voluminous universal relationships between states, yet these relationships are not only the originators but often also the evidence of existing law. The laws Great Britain and the United States need for their relations are not those required by Albania and Nicaragua in their relationship. The "individualized" nature of international law aggravates finding the law (and reduces the pressure for universalizing it through an international legislature).

There are also gray areas in the boundary region between a legally binding commitment and a political understanding. International relations abound with such understandings (for instance, between the United States and China not to cross certain lines during the Vietnam war; among the states possessing atomic weapons not to share them with others; between states to respect their spheres of influence). There is no criterion for a clear decision about the point at which such an understanding becomes a legal obligation.

The varying ways of "legislation" and forms of law mean a different applicability of law to different states. What is law for some states may not be law for others, even when states find themselves in the same situation. Depending upon the source in which the law is expressed or from whence it comes, some states may consider themselves bound, others not. The treatment of prisoners of war, for instance, can differ according to what source of law a state considers itself bound or not bound at all—a convention, general principles of humanitarianism, or customary law.

However, controversies between states arising from the decentralization of the sources are beginning to lose meaning as the globe is turning into one political action and therewith one law area. Law from all sources tends to have increasingly universal effect. Some states press for such an effect, others oppose it, and some do both depending upon their interests of the moment. Whatever they do, the trend does not seem to be much affected. Therefore, rather than being touched by laws they had no share in creating, especially the weaker states insist upon a share in the making of the laws. They are much more concerned about the effect of laws than about their source so that differentiations according to source begin to lose significance. Moreover, treaties are becoming such a predominant source of law (even though many merely codify previously existing rules) that most of the other sources are growing less and less relevant. One beneficial result is the gradual dissolution of the contrast between the dispersion of the sources of law and the unity of the globe as one law area. A further, more distant result may be, especially as multilateral treaties augment, that international law-making becomes an institutionalized activity.

The Globe—One Law Area

The common denominator of all rules of international law—universal or particular and whatever their source—is their function of maintaining social order in one international society in general by regulating various behaviors specifically. The integration of the rules is their overall, common purpose. This is the meaning of being a legal system. The rules are so interrelated that they complement each other toward their common purpose of social order;

that which affects one will affect the others. The same is true of their object, the international system, in which disorder anywhere is affecting order everywhere.

Both the legal and political international society have indeed become a system. Whatever happens somewhere is relevant elsewhere, regardless of the possibility that bilateral relations between some states are virtually absent. The mutual sensitivity among states can have a variety of reasons. They may be in contact through the United Nations. They may meet in multilateral conferences of wide scope. They may be related via the concern that some major powers may have in them. The subject matter of the law could concern them, such as the biosphere, nuclear explosions, or the weather. Or special interests may be shared by geographically separated states (as, for instance, interest in the resources of the sea is grouping widely separated countries together in the Law of the Sea conferences). In a world of interacting states even so-called particular (treaty) law tends to radiate a general effect upon its society. The International Court in the North Sea Continental Shelf case (1969: 41) found it "perfectly possible" that an article in a treaty may have the character of "a norm-creating provision which has constituted the foundation of, or has generated a rule which, while only conventional or contractual in its origin, has since passed into the general *corpus* of international law, and is now accepted as such by the *opinio juris,* so as to have become binding even for countries which have never and do not, become parties to the Convention."

The traditional subdivisions of international law according to source and kind are being overshadowed by the indivisibility of the world order. These distinctions are coming to mean little more than different ways of achieving the law's overall effect. It remains true that some laws command universal, others particular, obedience and that, of course, they are binding only when the conditions are fulfilled which the law envisages (e.g., laws relating to drivers apply only to those driving). The point is, however, that even when a law is binding only upon some states, for instance, those signing a convention, it nevertheless can create conditions other states have to respect. The new situation, though created by particular law, becomes part of the environment for all states. If, for instance, two states adjust their frontiers, other states cannot ignore the agreement; or, the existence of the United Nations is an important fact also for states who are not members. Any given law may affect a circle of states wider than those directly creating the law, both politically and legally. (This situation should not be confused with the situation in which a treaty specifically creates a right or an obligation for a third state not a party to the treaty.)

This efferent effect is an inevitable consequence of the order-maintaining mission of the law and the political oneness of the international society. Many of those states increasingly affected by laws in whose creation they had no share are therefore insisting upon having a role at least in the "legislative" international conferences. Their aim is expressed legally in a claim to participate in all multilateral treaties, or at least in those which either codify and develop norms of general international law or deal with matters of interest to the entire international society. The issue has led to a heated debate (summarized by Lukashuk, 1972 I: 292-321) over many years. It is conducted in terms of legal arguments which, however, cover only thinly the political interests of the parties. For many of the newer states, strongly supported by the Communist states, their participation in multilateral treaties is synonymous with an accretion to their political influence. The opposition by many of the older, major nations (such as the United States, Great Britain, and France) is, of course, based on a desire to frustrate such influence.

The Communist position was well summarized by the Soviet delegate in the General Assembly (United Nations, 1963b: 5-6) when he argued that a restriction of the right of participation is "nothing more than attempts to discriminate between various States. Such attempts run counter to the principle of the universality of multilateral international treaties. Objections to the general participation of States in treaties of this kind amount in fact to a denial of the principle of the sovereign equality of States." The main argument of the opposition is, of course, based on the same basic principle, but leading to the contrary conclusion, namely, that sovereignty entitles the parties to any treaty to determine who the parties to the treaty should be.[1] The rapporteur of a United Nations Committee dealing with the issue concluded, rather vaguely (United Nations, 1964b: 157), that all states should have the right to participate in the solution of international problems and in the formulation and amendment of the rules of international law.

The effect of these demands, if granted, would be to homogenize and generalize the sources of international law. The newer states want to eliminate those beyond their control and to strengthen those giving them a share in the creation of international law. The tendency would be toward developing a functional equivalent for a global legislature. But because it would remain a diplomatic conference rather than be a parliament, states rather than heads would continue to be counted. The political position of these newer states would be enhanced—which may explain why hitherto they have, at best, been moderately successful. The rejection by some important states of these demands means that the more traditional situation prevails. It remains therefore useful to consider the character and merits of at least customary and treaty law as the two most important current sources of international law, and the much less significant general principles of law as still relevant for some specific legal rules.

Customary Law

Custom is generally accepted as a source of international law, though with varying qualifications and enthusiasm by different states. Broadly speaking—the only level on which there is agreement—a custom is a regularly observed, continual, and repeated practice of states over a lengthy period of time. There is further widespread agreement that for a custom to turn into a legal rule, i.e., customary law, states must engage in the practice believing that it is their legal duty to do so. Customary law is defined by Judge Read of the International Court (Anglo-Norwegian Fisheries case, 1951: 191) as "the generalization of the practice of States." About its details, however, there is unending debate: what is a custom; when, why, and how does it turn into law; where can it be found; can it become universal law even if not all states practice it?

In several respects, customary law is well adapted to the international society. Custom is nearly identical with social reality. The distance between law and practice is short. Custom is living law. Custom also reflects the power constellation of the society, including the diffusion of power. Habitual behavior is likely to be the outcome of a political contest, with those in power having willed or at least tolerated the habitual behavior. The customary practice is in consonance with the society's power structure. Such coincidence of power and law is a prerequisite for the efficacy of law (though no guarantee of its justice). Because custom is also, by most definitions, behavior practiced by virtually all states in comparable situations, customary law tends to be universal law—unless the custom prevails only among a limited number of states and becomes particular customary law only for them. Finally, sovereignty and equality are safeguarded when all states participate in the custom. All these features making customary law widely acceptable and obeyed in principle also frequently ruin its attractiveness in practice.

The subjective element that states must believe the custom to be legally binding facilitates a state's escape from legal obligation. The close relation between the power structure and the law enables powerful states to undo customary behavior. Even weaker states by citing their sovereignty can readily disavow customary laws. Communist states selectively reject those rules which, they claim, were imposed by capitalist states upon the international society as "class law." A Soviet text on international law (Academy of the Sciences of the USSR, n.d.: 12) asserted that "Neglect for International Treaty Law and an exaggeration of the importance of international custom is characteristic of many bourgeois jurists. This is in line with the policy of certain imperialist circles, a policy of violating treaty obligations and giving legal form to illegal international practices under the label of 'international custom'."[2] Consequently, the Soviets emphasize treaty law as a much more important source. The Chinese Communists have been in a dilemma until recently. Their exclusion from international intercourse led them to underemphasize the importance of treaty law and to stress customary law. But customary law was "bourgeois" law mainly, hence largely unacceptable. As they are participating more in treaty making and international organization, their position is likely to parallel that of the Soviets.

The general suspicion of states in regard to rules of customary law—deriving from an intense dislike of having their freedom of action restrained by precedents of any kind—is particularly strong among the newer states. They were not in existence, they argue, when much customary law was born. Some of it was even part of the detested system in which colonialism flourished. Hence they are extremely cautious in recognizing rules of international customary law. An Algerian official insisted (United Nations, 1966d: 11; see also 1966b: 29) that "A general distinction should be drawn between an obligation voluntarily accepted and the general imposition of a law made in other times by a small international community." An Ecuadorian belittled customary law as having been "imposed by political power." And an Indian official welcomed attempts to codify the law of treaties as releasing states from the search for customary law, those "lawyer-based rules" which often gave only "a picture of what international law had been rather than what it actually is" (United Nations, 1968a: 3).

The International Court of Justice has frequently referred to customary law, although usually in a very careful manner and being very thorough in establishing the existence of specific rules, as, for instance, in the North Sea Continental Shelf and the Anglo-Norwegian Fisheries cases (see Jenks, 1964: 225-265; on customary law in general, see D'Amato, 1973).

The solidity and maturity of customary law is becoming its undoing in a highly dynamic and complex society. The long hardening process from habitual behavior and precedents into customary law makes this law more suitable for a steady society in which membership is large, change is slow, and innovations are rare. Its leisurely growth in a fast-moving world; the uncertainty of its existence in the face of changing relations; the doubtfulness of its existence and meaning when modern transactions need clarity and specificity are causes of its decline. Judge Alvarez of the International Court in the Anglo-Norwegian Fisheries case (1951: 36) pointed out that customs "tend to disappear as the result of rapid changes of modern international life; and a new case strongly stated may be sufficient to render obsolete an ancient custom. Customary law, to which such frequent reference is made in the course of the arguments, should therefore be accepted only with prudence."

The trend now appears to be to codify those rules of customary law, which are virtually universally acceptable because they regulate almost timeless and indispensable behavior in any society (e.g., treaties, diplomacy, sovereignty). Under the impact of new conditions in the contemporary society, customary law is falling behind. Social change demands a more adaptable method which conventional (treaty) law appears to supply.

Treaties

The greater popularity of treaties is, in part, due to their presumed greater clarity and evident presence as sources of law.

A treaty, or convention, agreement, and so forth, is a legal instrument in which the parties define mutual obligations and rights according to international law. These instruments are usually in written form. Any other form is also proper for creating binding commitments, provided that there is express evidence of their existence (see McNair, 1961; Bishop, 1971: 92-223; Vienna Convention on the Law of Treaties, 1969).

Among the advantages of treaties is that the commitments of the parties are explicit and the parties are known. The parties as well as other states know the legal situation. Sovereignty is preserved, yet does not stand in the way of making any subject matter the object of the treaty. In this manner states have converted a vast range of affairs hitherto of an "internal" or "domestic" character into international matters. Bilateral treaties and even more, treaties creating international agencies, now allow almost any aspect of human concern and interest to be discussed internationally. Treaties thus help in giving states the opportunity to specify issues of mutual concern through legal formulation; clarifying the relationship of their interests; organizing their interactions; relegating ideological and value differences into irrelevancies; and, above all, correlating their power to the extent of their agreement.

The explication of contacts between states in treaties could diminish tensions. In any case, when the need is for the ordering of a multiplicity of contacts among states and the regulation of specific functions, treaty law is readily available, adjustable to detailed needs, applicable to states of the most diverse character, and able to keep pace with the dynamics of the international society. Multilateral treaties assist in universalizing international law by having many signatories, by allowing states to accede to the treaties, or by creating precedents affecting all other states (Parry [1965: 28-55] and others deny that treaties are a source).

Treaties have their drawbacks as well, especially from the standpoint of developing the volume and efficacy of international law. A treaty represents a bargain, but it may be a very unsatisfactory one when it reflects great inequality between the partners and their uneven power relationship. The degree of voluntarism on the part of the signatories can vary widely and therewith their intensity of adherence to the treaty. The conditions of the international society allow each party to bring the totality of its power to bear upon the other, unrelated as that may be to the issue of the treaty. Peace treaties are the most extreme example of such a possibility. There are less extreme examples in the forms of unequal treaties from which, for instance, China has suffered in the past and over which many smaller states continue to be restless and fearful.

Differences in the power potential between treaty partners can be particularly obnoxious because the rejection of a treaty obligation is difficult. The reason is not so much inability as unwillingness to reject. States consider it good politics to fulfill treaties. As John Stuart Mill once pointed out (1870), it may be more immoral forcing a state to adhere to a treaty than letting a state reject it. But a state refusing to honor a treaty is likely to be branded untrustworthy and dishonorable, and for good reason. Keeping treaties is a fundamental necessity for orderly social life; and ostracism of a state breaking them easily is an important sanction. States are therefore careful before committing themselves. They are clear in specifying their obligations; they are precise about the forms of fulfillment. The conclusion, maintenance, interpretation, suspension, invalidity, and ending of treaties have received much consideration by states. Agreement has been such that the codification of the law of treaties is a most successful attempt by many to codify international law.

But that success did not include a solution to the problem of the contradictory character of treaties. They are a good means for keeping law "living," but they also always run the risk of becoming dead letters. Once a state has entered a treaty commitment, there is no easy escape from it. Yet unforeseeable conditions can arise, or the situation and environment in which a treaty was born can change so radically that a party to the treaty can hardly be expected to keep it. The political and legal systems of the international society provide at best inadequate methods for coping with such a situation, so that oftentimes states are forced to employ methods for changing or ending treaties which are highly undesirable for the social order. They have used superior power to terminate a treaty; they have insisted on giving it irresistible unilateral interpretations; they have arbitrarily accused their partner of having broken the treaty to be themselves released from it. They have, in other words, used political means disguised as legal principles to escape their commitments.

The problem involved is how to cope with social change. Specifically, the problem is how to reconcile the need for regular and predictable behavior with the irregular and unpredictable development of the international society. The conserving nature of law must be matched with the mobility of social conditions. New treaties are quite suitable for taking care of the first side of the need, but, as they grow older, not of the second. The distance between a treaty and social reality can become great quickly. Lack of a community spirit, placing the quality of the group above fulfillment of sectional (state) interests in the international society, prevents that society from coping with the problem in any satisfactory manner, satisfactory, that is, to the vast majority of its members. If social change is not to cause constant upheavals, the solution of the problem can never be found in a completely adequate legal measure alone. That, at least, is the conclusion from attempts made so far in this direction.

Social Change

The function of law as making behavior predictable limits its usefulness as a tool for change. It can more often slow down or prevent than promote change. If law is to remain living its task is to countervail politics as the primary means of change by fixing the manner in which politics may function and by delimiting the adjustments and adaptations politics can be allowed to produce. Law is thus not a barrier to change; it aims at making change stable. This interplay between law and politics produces a stable and peaceful society. A good illustration of its operation is the conversion of a political understanding, e.g., a tacitly agreed modus vivendi, into a legal commitment. The instability of the international society results from politics untamed by law. But law is ill-equipped to produce a balance, and to burden it with that task is not merely bound to be unsuccessful, it also causes disrespect for the law. In any society stability must result from all the institutions of the entire society. In the international society the inadequacy of law to guarantee stability is enhanced because the same factors weakening the law also cause politics to lack elements that, in national societies, help to make change stable and peaceful. The sense of community, the citizen's socialization, the social controls, the outlets for public opinion, the articulation and expression of desires for change are all underdeveloped and their institutionalization almost absent. Justice, always strongly involved in social change, is especially controversial in international relations. Max Huber remarked in 1919 that a state "possesses in its legislature a regulative organ which normally ensures the adaptation of the law to the changing conditions of power within a society, whereas the essentially contractual nature of the relations of independent States enables States interested in the maintenance of the *status quo* to prevent or obstruct the evolution of the law."[3]

The international society has tried to cope with the problem for a long time. The clausula rebus sic stantibus may be invoked by a party to a treaty in order to be released from its commitment. The condition is that certain circumstances present or foreseen at the time the treaty was concluded must have changed so fundamentally that a party cannot reasonably be held to the treaty any longer. Article 19 of the League of Nations Covenant incorporated a similar principle. Article 14 of the United Nations Charter broadens the principle to include "any situation" which may impair the general welfare or friendly relations among nations and charges the General Assembly with making recommendations for a peaceful adjustment, thus transferring the problem into the political forum where it belongs.

The discussions during the Vienna Conference on the Law of Treaties defined the problem very clearly, without finding a new solution (see United Nations, 1968: 378-382; 1963c: 249-256). Agreement was reached that the clausula rebus sic stantibus had to be introduced "to serve the real purpose of the law, which was to preserve today's way of life" (United Nations, 1963c: 254). But there was agreement also that if treaty obligations were to be voided for specific reasons, an impartial determination was essential, yet none such was achievable in the international society (United Nations, 1968: 406, 407). The International Law Commission expressed consensus in its preparatory work for the Treaties Conference when it stated that jurists had reluctantly accepted the clausula but "at the same time enter a strong *caveat* as to the need to confine the scope of the doctrine within narrow limits and to regulate strictly the conditions under which it may be invoked" (United Nations, 1969a: 118).

The final formulation is in Article 62 of the Vienna Convention on the Law of Treaties. "A fundamental change of circumstances which has occurred with regard to those existing at the time of the conclusion of a treaty, and which was not foreseen by the parties, may not be invoked as a ground for terminating or withdrawing from the treaty unless: (a) the existence of those circumstances constituted an essential basis of the consent of the parties to be bound by the treaty; and (b) the effect of the change is radically to transform the extent of obligations still to be performed under the treaty . . . ."

In addition to this principle states can invoke, they increasingly introduce into the treaty itself certain conditions under which the parties are released from it. Especially in treaties dealing with economic matters formulae such as "serious disequilibrium" or "fundamental disturbances" are agreed as reasons for ending or suspending the treaty.

Whatever the principle invoked by a state for releasing it from treaty commitments, states are cautious in using it lest frequent practice would make treaties useless. When the clausula has been invoked in several cases, the major change was not in the conditions underlying the conclusion of the treaty but in the relative power positions of the signatories, enabling the more powerful party to denounce the treaty successfully (Schwarzenberger, 1967: 169-170). Invocation of the clausula served to make political behavior appear legal.

General Principles of Law

A third, minor source of international law, also admitted in the Statute of the International Court of Justice, is "the general principles of law recognized by civilized nations." These are principles of national legal systems sufficiently widespread among states to serve as a foundation for the deduction of specific legal norms.[4] This source has proved useful in many arbitration cases and in some cases before the International Court of Justice. Among the principles or their derivatives used to support judgments and awards have been abuse of rights; liability for damage resulting from a breach of obligation; responsibility for the consequences of hazardous actions; and the effect of error on the validity of treaties.

Outside the judicial and arbitration processes, general principles of law as originators of international legal norms have played an even less important role. States refer to them—when they do at all—in general terms and more for political than for legal reasons. They use them to prove the righteousness of their cause and their concern for law. They refer to them in justification of conventions creating new international law, such as the Genocide Convention or the London Agreement of 1945 for the Prosecution of European Axis War Criminals. New states have demonstrated with their help the anachronism of certain legal norms, especially those legitimizing colonialism or the consequences of inequality. These principles have also been cited in mixed contracts of a partly private, partly public nature (e.g., the private oil companies with Arab governments; private corporations involved with governments in developing states). Mostly, states have ignored these general principles in formulating their treaties or settling their disputes.

The advantages of this source of law are, first, that if it can be discovered and agreed upon, it is instantly available and for unique situations. And second, the role of the judges or arbitrators can be more creative than usual in deriving specific norms from general principles. They are not limited to any particular legal system; and they may either adapt general principles to the requirements of the given case, or they may formulate new norms.

The disadvantages of this source are, however, considerable, which may explain why the International Court especially has been reluctant to rely on it (Jenks, 1964: 266-315; Stone, 1974: 59-67). The conceptualization of the source in the Statute raises problems similar to those found in connection with customary law. So much interpretation is needed before norms can be derived from principles that political manipulation will have interfered long before acceptable legal methods will have led to appropriate conclusions agreeable to all parties. Moreover, the effectiveness of the Court depends almost entirely on the cooperation of the parties. Basing its decisions upon uncertain principles endangers the acceptability of its judgments. There is always the need to appease those states insisting that sovereignty guarantees freedom of action in the absence of definite norms limiting such freedom. The Court therefore prefers to rely upon principles and norms of international law more unquestionably accepted by states. Finally, the range of legal systems in the contemporary international society from which general principles could be culled is wide. The parties to a case would obviously opt for the one most favorable to their cause. The precarious situation of the Court would not be helped if the judges had to get involved in such a controversy.

The reluctance of states to expose their case to the vagaries of general principles and the norms to which these might lead is understandable also in the light of the wider relationship between national legal systems and international law. These general principles of national legal systems are to be transferred directly or by analogy to the international legal system (Lauterpacht, 1970). But the moral, ideological, or legal principles underlying the national systems are not necessarily those underlying the international legal system. States can hardly be expected, when acting on the international scene, to submit to such transferred principles in general, and especially not in view of the fact that very often the social behavior within states differs greatly from that in international relations. "My country right or wrong" illustrates the situation. The liberties taken by governments for reasons of state externally would often be considered intolerable when taken internally. For instance, that nobody can be a judge in his own case is a widely accepted general principle of law among "civilized states." Yet sovereignty guarantees that states can be judges in their own cases.

States will not readily subject themselves to norms based upon legal principles taken from a national system which are out of context in the international society. Legal principles are part of a legal system which is itself an integral part of a social system in which it may function very well as a subsystem. But transferred to another social system, they may be quite incongruent and not function at all. This possibility is not a matter of different national cultures existing side by side in the international society and possibly having each a legal system incompatible with that of all the others. It is, instead, a matter of the international society having its own culture and character, differing from all national cultures, and therefore needing a legal system and legal principles peculiarly its own.

These disadvantages and difficulties of general legal principles as a source of international legal norms notwithstanding, it may assume some importance in the future. Acculturation, especially the acceptance by developing countries of institutions from more developed countries, will also affect the correlated legal principles and norms. Much of the time, specific laws go with specific institutions, not with a national culture in general. Whoever adopts the institutions is likely to adopt their legal regulation. The introduction of a credit card system, for instance, will include its legal regulation, which is not likely to differ much from country to country. The empirical evidence is that where the fulfillment of an interest required joint international pursuit, states have not failed to agree on the necessary legal regulation.

The relative importance of these sources is subject to variations. Changing conditions of international existence cause shifts in the emphasis on sources. What they all have in common is their reflection of power relations. But their usefulness depends to a large extent upon the manner in which power finds expression in international relations at any given period. When interaction was minimal, when relations were essentially "political," and mutual interest more often clashing than not, customary law was more adequate than in a later period. As all societies in more recent times turn from political into welfare and economic societies, which means that states are expected to perform many more functions for their citizens, their mutual interests are better served by cooperation than by conflict and violence. They are, therefore, also better served by treaty than by any other law. The multiplication of international interests facilitates the control of power, at least in the sense of moving the terminal point of conflict back from violence. At the same time the growth of international (conventional) law is thereby also assured. Expanding wants and needs of states internationalize much subject matter, enhancing the value of bargaining and diminishing the value of force as tools of power.

The Utility of Treaty Law

When states meet, as they did customarily in the past, as sovereign equals and as entities, when they confront each other in their totality on all occasions, regardless of the particulars in a given case, their differences in power are very relevant. No matter what one state may want from another, each always can and often does bring its total power potential to bear on the issue. States can use means of pressure not at all related to the issue. A state, for instance, might want a raw material from an underdeveloped country and can use the threat to withhold aid if it cannot get the material on its terms. The Arab states shut off the supply of oil to enforce a certain policy by the United States toward Israel. These matters are related to each other only because states confront each other as entities.

More recently and with expanding contacts and mutual needs, states approach each other more selectively according to the complementarity of their specific interests and resources. The sum total of their differences in power potentials becomes less prominent and influential. They meet specifically on the basis of what one has to offer the other. If they can come to an agreement, particular law will be created. Their differences will still be effective at least in the background. But the more diversified each state's interests and needs become the greater is the opportunity for developing selective relations and therewith for creating additional particular law in which inequalities will be less relevant.

The internationalization of an increasing volume of subject matter is favorable to the growth of international law also because it interweaves national and international relations. More and more public and private interests, whether originating on the national or international scene, require international action for their satisfaction. This linkage between internal and external affairs is breaking down barriers to interaction erected by sovereignty. The functional unity of a chain of actions undertaken to satisfy some interest (e.g., the functional relations between the buyer of bread, the baker baking it, the miller grinding the flour, the farmer growing the wheat, the manufacturer producing the fertilizer, and so forth) is anathema to divisive organization. When this chain of action involves international transactions, sovereignty is experienced by those benefitting from the transactions, as a handicap to the achievement of a desired goal. They may still want it as nationalists, but they do not want it as a consumer of bread, a baker, and so on.

But all social relations extend over time, space, and usually numerous individuals needing organization. Different parts of these relations may be subject to different organizational jurisdictions. Administratively they can fall within the bailiwick of a city, county, or state. They may also be subdivided substantively, belonging to the areas of economics, politics, and religion. These different jurisdictions and subdivisions are presumably intended to be organizational conveniences, to serve social coordination and coexistence, to help public order, to further the citizens' purposes, and, ultimately, to lead to an integrated society. The functional unity of social relationships is presumably to be assisted, not hampered. All this is true, at least, in national societies.

As soon as these functionally unified relations extend across national borders, their unity is interrupted. They are no longer contained within a social system whose very purpose is to further these relations. Even the quality of the organizational institutions and the subdivisions changes. They are no longer merely means or facilities to make these relations possible. Some become ends themselves. The state, for instance, is no longer there to help advance functional relationships. It is an end in itself. The relations which were initiated for certain functional purposes, for instance, to get wheat from one country to a miller in another, suddenly are ascribed different or additional goals as they extend across national borders. Suddenly, they not only serve their original purpose, but also are used by the state for its purposes, quite independently of the original purpose. The wheat may be withheld from the other country for political, noneconomic reasons. The state evaluates these relations not only on their own terms from the viewpoint of their primary, initial function, but also and first from the national viewpoint of sovereignty, security, and power potential. If these relations pass muster there, they are allowed to serve their original purpose. Music lovers in Moscow and New York may wish to hear each other's major symphony orchestras, but before they can do so, the two states involved will examine the political advisability of exchanging these orchestras.

The state's considerations are extraneous, usually, to the original purposes for which the relations were initiated. It does not aim at furthering these relations in the light of their original purposes, but to further or interrupt them for the state's national purposes. This break at the national borders is further emphasized by the fact that suddenly these relations become subject to a different legal system. To the individuals involved, all this is of great disadvantage. Their interests have not changed and all the relations initiated to satisfy them have not changed. From the sociological and functional standpoint the network of relations tying people together, wherever they may live and whatever passports they may carry, consists of an uninterrupted chain more or less according to the principle that one thing always leads to another, increasingly so in an age of high division of labor.

Substantively these relations are interconnected. But men may divide them into national and international, internal and external, economic and political. Their functional linkage remains intact. Yet these quite artificial subdivisions, separations, and categorizations seem unable to withstand the strength of the interests producing the relations in the first place—providing the interests are strong enough. Contemporary interests seem to be sufficiently strong so that states can no longer fully control all the relations existing across national borders. The interests, leading to the relations for their fulfillment, seem to become stronger than the influence of the jealously guarded sovereignty. The interests seeking satisfaction can less and less be contained by reference to difficulties and limits created by national boundaries. The multitude of international organizations, the large number of flourishing private international organizations, and the innumerable treaties now in existence indicate that the demand for the satisfaction of interests ignores whence these satisfactions come or what legal systems control them. Instead of worrying about types of law and hierarchies among legal systems, these interests press for legal regulations to safeguard their satisfaction—and they usually get them. Hence the rapid growth of particular international law. This process tends to feed upon itself under modern conditions. New interests lead to more relations and more relations stimulate new interests. Law is bound to follow. The prospect is that particular international law will keep growing and rapidly so as functional relations across the globe increase.

Time will tell whether the qualitative and quantitative change in the nature of international relations will be beneficial to the growth and strength of international law. Against the various projections just outlined must be held the continuing fascination with sovereignty in most national societies. If the newer states appear more attached to sovereignty and have a more extreme interpretation of it, the reason may be that for them it is a possible safeguard of their independent existence. It also could be a necessary element in nation-building and a gradually waning reaction to colonialism and suppression in the past.

Yet these states too are aware of indispensable international interaction if they are to be viable states. Under contemporary conditions this means inevitably a moderate application of sovereignty in deeds and a facilitation of creating international law. The positions taken by these states at the United Nations Conference on Trade and Development, for instance, show their ambivalence toward the international society and its law. The new states cannot avoid a growing involvement in relations with other states and the accompanying consequence of growing international law. They seem willing, some more reluctantly than others, to accept this necessity, provided they have a share in the formulation of new international law and a right of acquiescence in the old. This demand, joined with the changing nature of international interaction, places emphasis on treaties as the major source of law. The problem of creating law to match the speed of social change becomes thereby easier to solve. But the problem of slowing the rapidity with which laws get out of date becomes more difficult. The solution of that problem is political rather than legal. The contribution the legal system can make is to safeguard the orderliness of the political process through which new conditions and their legal regulation are absorbed by the society.

NOTES

1. The issue of participation in multilateral treaties has often been discussed in the United Nations and its various agencies. See, e.g., the Yearbooks of the International Law Commission, United Nations (1957: 157-158; 1965a: 113-143; 1965b: 72), or the Commission's sessions on the Law of Treaties, United Nations (1965c: 106; 1965d: 205-213).

2. The expedient use of customary law by the Soviets was highlighted during the Third United Nations Conference on the Law of the Sea (United Nations, 1974e: 68) when their delegate stated, in regard to straits which might come under the sovereignty of a state: "The conclusion to be drawn from the established practice of navigation in international straits was that a rule of common law had already been established, recognizing the right of transit through such straits for all ships."

3. Huber is quoted in Lauterpacht (1933: 246). On international law and social change, see Weber (1960: 51-83), Friedmann (1964: 117-151; 1972: 17-90, 443-492), and Landheer (1957 I: 62-79).

4. Soviet writers interpret this source to be only general principles of international, not of municipal, law (Tunkin, 1974: 195-203). The opposite opinion, supported here, is considered an attempt to foist capitalist principles of law upon the international society and an attack upon the Communist and the new states of Asia and Africa. Chinese Communist theory is unclear. Chinese official documents refer occasionally to "general principles of international law" by which they appear to mean existing international, not municipal, law (see Kaminski, 1973: 182-185).

Chapter 6

THE SUBJECTS OF INTERNATIONAL LAW

Sovereignty in orthodox form requires that only states can be formal creators and beneficiaries of international law. As subjects of international law, only states had rights, duties, and responsibilities for a long time. Emmerich de Vattel expressed this idea as full autonomy internally and therefore full independence externally. But when Hugo Grotius surveyed international law, he argued that it covered relations between states as well as between individuals subject to different national jurisdictions.

No individual or social unit possesses inherent qualities determining suitability or unsuitability for subjectivity under international law. Any unit can be a subject if the international society so decides. The International Court of Justice, in the Reparations for Injuries case (1949: 178), said that "The subjects of law in any legal system are not necessarily identical in their nature or in the extent of their rights, and their nature depends upon the needs of the community. Throughout its history, the development of international law has been influenced by the requirements of international life, and the progressive increase in the collective activities of States has already given rise to instances of action upon the international plane by certain entities which are not States." But it does not follow that an actor on the international scene subject to the law must also be a maker of that law.

Nationalism has caused states to reject Grotius' findings. They have also resisted the pressure from changing requirements of international life for sharing with other, new social entities their subjectivity under international law. They made themselves, in the name of sovereignty, the exclusive repositories of international legal jurisdiction and seem quite determined to maintain their privilege. Until very recently they claimed and obtained complete legal control over individuals and collectivities. With a few exceptions, such as pirates, diplomats, blockade runners, and certain criminals, international law did not deal directly with individuals or groups other than states. If international law wished to reach them, or if they wished to reach international law, their state had to be the intermediary. In international law, the individual is the forgotten man.

The Permanent Court of International Justice (in the Mavrommatis case) and the International Court of Justice (in the Nottebohm case) have held that when a state takes judicial action on behalf of its citizens, it does so not to satisfy any citizen's right but to satisfy its own interests in the maintenance of international law. Ultimately, of course, international law, like all law, deals with human beings. But it deals with them in a special way: not as individuals in their own right, but as members of a collectivity, the state, to which a fictitious personality is ascribed. States are agreed upon this arrangement as an internal and external political necessity—regardless of the political régime prevailing within their borders.

With the declining majesty and exclusivity of the state, this arrangement is also very slowly eroding. Wishful thinking among writers and a few judges of the International Court makes them perceive, in their enthusiasm for an improved international law, much sharing of subjectivity by states with other entities, especially international organizations, when, in fact, states have at best made some minor concessions hesitantly and only occasionally. Such perceptions are sometimes based upon a confusion between agencies other than states stimulating the growth of new law and the actual creation of new law. In such situations, a good test is to ascertain where the ultimate power to make law is located. It will usually be found that the power to make laws by these agencies is derived from states and that, in general, agreement among states is still the basic requirement for the birth of new law.

States as Subjects

States continue to play their roles as major, virtually exclusive subjects of international law with great tenacity. Two reasons are mainly responsible. People in their nationalist ardor want them to play that role; and there are some practical advantages to it.

The state fulfills many psychic needs of its citizens. Nationalism remains a powerful emotion, able to evoke the highest sacrifices. The inherent value of the state as a community to large sections of its citizenry can explain its central place in international politics and law. People have also convinced themselves on the basis of an expedient misunderstanding that the coexistence of states in sovereign independence is justice. The misunderstanding, especially widespread among the newer states, lies in identifying legal equality with democratic justice: one nation, one vote. The underlying erroneous assumption is that democracy is designed for collectivities when in fact it deals with individuals, when its very task is to protect individuals against submergence in collective entities. One vote for India and one for the United States is not democracy. Six hundred million and 220 million votes, respectively, is. Indeed, the misunderstanding (if such it is) serves to frustrate democratic purposes by saving governments from outside interference if they proceed undemocratically against their own citizens. Sovereignty protects states against the collective will—as expressed in international law—of the international society in their domestic affairs. States can, for instance, sign the Universal Declaration of Human Rights and at the same time use torture against their own prisoners (as more than half of the signatories do, according to the International Commission of Jurists).

A practical advantage of states remaining major political entities in the world is organizational neatness. The globe is divided into definable, territorially based units. This result is, of course, a byproduct of people wanting states. But it is useful because it clarifies where one unit ends and another begins, what one unit may do or not do to another. Not surprisingly, international law is relatively best developed in regard to making this global division specific: regulating frontiers, acquisition and loss of territory, control over nationals, responsibilities of states toward each other. Citizens can know with fair certainty the boundaries of their cherished community. The division is neat physically and psychologically.[1] Some grey areas, not decisively settled by accepted rules (such as protectorates, trust territories, the Holy See, insurgent régimes, international organizations, the moon, or multinational corporations) are as yet too insignificant to upset the basic arrangement. The international legal system so far has been able to absorb them without having to make fundamental concessions on either the role of states as subjects of international law or the division of the globe into national units.

The independence of states is valuable also as a safeguard of international law, paradoxical as that may seem. The more independent states there are the greater is the opportunity for creating and maintaining balances of power (under most definitions of that controversial concept). With a balance of power as one of the more important guarantees of the binding power of law, a multiplicity of states becomes desirable for selfish national reasons as long as the existence of every state depends to some extent upon the rule of law.

The services of the state to emotion and practicality would diminish if other public or private agencies were allowed to compete with states as subjects of international law. The refusal to break their monopoly thus becomes a matter of self-preservation for states. This phenomenon is noticeable even in Western Europe where, with the approach of the deadline for political integration, the once strong intention of reducing the exclusivity of states is weakening. Typically, European community consensus and the requisite institutions have advanced most in the economic sphere and least in the political spheres of European legislation, diplomacy, and security.

In the past the question of states' sharing subjectivity in international law was not very acute. There were few entities able to compete with states in potential or need of becoming subjects. There were a few instances of exceptions to the general principle. Administrative international units, such as river commissions, were granted limited international personality. Individuals could occasionally deal under special treaties with states before international tribunals for purposes of reparation for damages. In the Universal Postal Union territories or certain geographic areas, not fully states, were admitted as members for practical purposes. When problems arose, they were usually solved in favor of the state's monopoly. Thus, the United States, for instance, refused to admit in 1929, and again in 1959, that either "the International Red Cross" or the Sovereign Order of Malta were to be treated like states or given international personality (Bishop, 1971: 303-304).

Individuals, Organizations, and Corporations as Other Subjects

What was practical, reasonable, possible, or even useful, and cherished many decades ago does not appear to be so any longer. Attitudes toward the state are changing, affecting the possibility of maintaining states as isolated entities. The international political system is bound to be touched by this development and therefore so is international law—not dramatically, but steadily.

Citizens question the supremacy of the state. In their eyes it is transforming from an untouchable object of worship into a tool for the promotion of material welfare. Its officers are therefore no longer holding their positions by divine right and no "higher will" can immunize them against criticism. They are appointed and subject to recall. They cannot even escape their responsibility by hiding behind "orders from above" (Nürnberg, Tokyo, My Lai). As a guarantor of security the state is losing some confidence with its public. It has become penetrable, even if it is among the strongest, by being physically vulnerable and economically dependent.

Some of the state's most attractive features for its citizens—providing safety and material welfare—are no longer its monopoly. Instead or additionally, international public organizations or private groups are rendering these services. As a consequence, states find it increasingly difficult to justify their insistence upon exclusivity. They continue to resist the usurpation of their role by other agencies, and fairly successfully so far. But they are under continuous pressure to delegate, and perhaps eventually to abandon, more and more the reality of their authority and decision-making power to international bodies.

The process is taking place somewhat haphazardly and piecemeal—but it exists. In international conferences dealing with international law there is much talk—though little action—of subjects of international law other than states (e.g., United Nations, 1950: 1; 1953: 4, 14, 21; 1956: 14; 1962a: 26; 1966j: 20; 1968: 12, 13, 15, 16, 59; 1962b; 1966i: 294, 325). The International Court of Justice in the Reparations for Injuries case (1949: 179; confirmed in the South-West Africa case, second phase, 1966: 30) examined the characteristics of the United Nations, comparing them with those of states. It reached the conclusion "that the Organization is an international person. That is not the same thing as saying that it is a State, which it certainly is not, or that its legal personality and rights and duties are the same as those of a State. . . . What it does mean is that it is a subject of international law and capable of possessing international rights and duties, and that it has capacity to maintain its rights by bringing international claims." The Court went even further by asserting that once a collectivity such as the United Nations had become a subject of international law, the individual member states had lost the jurisdiction which they had granted the organization. A similar arrangement exists for the civil servants of the European community. They may be proposed by their governments but once appointed are entirely under the jurisdiction of the community and obligated not to be guided by considerations of national interests of their home states.

None of these situations lends itself to generalizations. The International Court made this clear in regard to its decision, but it is true also in all other cases. Every international organization is sui generis. Whether it has international personality and to what extent depends upon its constitution. They depend, that is to say, upon the willingness of the member states to grant such personality. The personality is thus dependent upon and a derivative of states as subjects of international law. States have discretion over the nature of the grant they agree to make and, for that matter, also over the withdrawal of such a grant.

Once international organizations or other entities have been granted personality, they may, of course, act on that basis, influence the development of international law, and generally create an environment in which freedom of action and decision of their creator states is reduced. But such "auto-limitation" is nothing new in international law and has never been considered to affect the exclusivity of states as subjects of international law.

The experience so far has been that states make grants of legal personality most stingily. It was typical that the United Nations Conference on the Law of Treaties excluded from its codification treaties concluded by international organizations because these "have many special characteristics; and the [International Law] Commission considered that it would unduly complicate matters and delay drafting of the present articles if it were to attempt to include in them satisfactory provisions concerning international organizations." Most nations supporting this position argued that customary law on treaties between states was sufficiently mature to be codified, but that the same could not be said of treaties concluded by international organizations (United Nations, 1966j: 20). Inofficially, it was explained that behind this argument was a fear that to give international organizations a codified right to conclude treaties might once remove treaty-making power from states and too many states found the thought intolerable.

The individual occupies an even more disadvantageous place in international law—or almost none at all (see Friedmann, 1964: 232-249; Bishop, 1971: 460-465; McDougal, Lasswell, and Reisman, 1967: 261-275). Should he become a subject of international law, the state as a subject may indeed wither away. The same applies, in principle, to international private organizations, specifically the multinational corporations. For this reason, neither has made noticeable progress in playing a role in international law in its own right. Only occasionally have international nongovernmental organizations obtained a slightly favorable position, namely, when they were given consultant status in the Economic and Social Council of the United Nations and in several specialized agencies.[2]

The principle still holds that the individual, alone or in private groupings, is dependent upon his state for rights, duties, or responsibilities incumbent upon him from international law. In the vast majority of the situations—of which the international Covenants on Human Rights are typical and symbolic—states must implement individually whatever they have agreed on collectively. Exceptionally, there have been cases in which individuals were direct beneficiaries of international agreements. The Permanent Court of International Justice in the case of the Jurisdiction of the

Courts of Danzig (1928: 31-32) confirmed in a "revolutionary" pronouncement (Lauterpacht) that "an international agreement cannot, as such, create direct rights and obligations for private individuals." But having stated that, the Court proceeded to say that "the very object of an international agreement, according to the intention of the contracting Parties, may be the adoption of the Parties of some definite rules creating individual rights and obligations and enforceable by the national courts" (cf. also Lauterpacht, 1934: 173-176). In the opinion of the Court then, individuals may be direct beneficiaries of international agreements. The United Nations Charter in Article 80 speaks of the rights of states and peoples, and so did the International Court of Justice in the International Status of South-West Africa case. After World War I, the victorious nations forced the defeated nations into arbitration tribunals where individuals could sue states for damages. In the same postwar situation some individuals and minority groups gained certain rights against states in Upper Silesia. In the International Labor Organization employer and employee groups participate directly in the deliberations of the organization. On occasion, special interest groups are allowed to appear and plead before international agencies. Finally, private persons who wish to safeguard their rights under community law can be parties before the European Court of Justice. Whether these exceptions indicate a trend is unpredictable. The behavior of states so far has not encouraged any belief that they do. States are not likely to abandon political control over their citizens if they can possibly help it.

The situation is different regarding corporations. Two contradictory pressures affect developments. The need of many, especially developing, states to enter into agreements with corporations favors granting corporations the capacity to be subjects of international law. The growing importance of economics as a political tool and instrument of power works in the opposite direction. States will not readily forego the usefulness of corporations as political tools by giving them the right to be their own international personalities. The legal situation is in flux. Whether, for instance, agreed arbitration between a state and a corporation brings the state to the level of a "private" person or turns the corporation into an international person can be debated often but inconclusively. Disputes between states and corporations have been dealt with by courts in a very specific, detailed manner so that generalizations can hardly be made. Conceivably, the exclusive subjectivity of states may be affected by an increasing number of such mixed agreements in the future. In the meantime, the exalted status of the state continues, and the essence and basic principles of international law regarding who is its subject remain unchanged.

The State as "Personality"

Treatment of the state as a collectivity with personality has proved troublesome (see Tucker, 1966: 245-246, 573-574; Scelle, 1932 I: 9-13). The state is a mental concept. Its reality is in its individual citizens interacting in a certain fashion. But anthropomorphication is common practice in daily language. Concepts like labor union, university, and government are used as if they were living creatures and for certain purposes usefully so. For the state anthropomorphication has some justification because nationalists do worship the state as such. Their emotions are not normally invested in all the individual citizens of their country; they are invested in the collectivity. The nationalist identifies with his country as an abstraction to which he ascribes superior qualities (which, as far as individuals are concerned, at most may be symbolized by some individual heroes).

Fortunately for the political role states as entities insist upon playing, legal systems have no difficulties in dealing with fictitious or "juristic" persons: corporations, foundations, cities, counties, and so forth. A number of theories have been developed to rationalize this practice. The existence of "corporate personalities" has been argued. An "organic theory" has been expounded, treating the state as a living organism. A collectivity has been postulated as something new and different from its component individuals—a "communal ghost" as Morris Cohen (1931: 386) called it derogatorily.

The international society has solved the problem in a pragmatic fashion. International law deals with states as if they were persons as far as possible. International documents speak frequently of a state's personality that other states must not violate or a state is entitled to preserve. The entire citizenry is presumed to benefit from rights and to be obligated toward the performance of duties. Government officials are treated as representatives of their states, having (with very few exceptions) no personal responsibilities toward other states. The law determines that the social legal consequences and effects of the will and actions of the state's representatives shall accrue to those "represented," i.e., normally the entire population.

The principle of the state as a personality has created problems in practical application. What, for instance, is permissible self-defense of a state? When is the social "life" of a group threatened and how is such life to be defined? How can a collective personality be violated? Who represents the collectivity and when does he act in his representative and when in his personal capacity? International law has answers to these problems. It tries to define self-defense. On representation it has taken the position that only subjects of international law can break international law (an approach bound to become complicated as entities other than states are becoming subjects). International law dealing with states as personalities has not created major difficulties because peoples everywhere support the practice emotionally. Law expressed what the international society holds to be the desired and necessary relationships between states (see Laski, 1948: 55). Citizens readily submerge themselves into their state as a unit in international relations. They are agreeable to letting their state be the carrier of rights, duties, and responsibilities in relations with other states, and to accepting the consequences collectively.

FUNDAMENTAL RIGHTS OF STATES

The supremacy of the state is legally fixed in the concept of sovereignty. The meaning is that, with the exceptions already noted, states are the only official actors in the international society;[3] that only actions undertaken by states can formally commit them politically or legally; that states cannot be legally bound against their will; that states are equal in law and have only one voice in voting situations; that no state may violate the territorial, political, and, maybe, cultural integrity of another state; and that no state may interfere in the domestic affairs of another.

A panel of the Permanent Court of Arbitration summed up these rights by saying that "Sovereignty in the relation between States signifies independence" (Scott, 1932: 92). This principle of the exclusive competence of the State, the panel continued, has become during the last few centuries "the point of departure in settling most questions that concern international relations . . . ."

The principle is cherished by all states as a guarantee of their personality and supremacy. Paradoxically, it enables the more powerful states to undermine exactly that supremacy of the weaker states. There is no assurance that this legal principle can prevent damaging political attacks by one state upon another, or, for that matter, by influential private interests of foreign origin (e.g., multinationals) that may not even be subject to international law. Weak states are fully aware of this situation, hence their eternal and enthusiastic attempts to expand the principle of sovereignty while simultaneously trying to restrain politics with legal rules. If their territorial and formal political sovereignty appears more secure at present than several decades ago the reason must be found in changing instruments of power and methods of politics rather than in the success of their particular attempts. The political domination powerful states have always sought to attain can be achieved under contemporary conditions by nonviolent means which, indeed, enhance in some ways the usefulness of international law. But this possibility should not lead to the illusion that powerful states have abandoned their political ambitions.

RECOGNITION

The importance of states requires certainty about what a state is and the legitimacy of its government. The international society handles these questions under the rubric of recognition, indicating that the answers are not based on objective facts but on subjective acts of state. Fairly objective criteria could be established to determine whether there is a state or the identity of the state's government. The International Court of Justice could play an important role in this enterprise. But the international society has never approached the situation in any objective fashion, notwithstanding the usual pretense by states that their recognitions of states and governments are not affected by subjective evaluations or political considerations. Only the United States finally admitted in recognizing Israel and later in dealing with the People's Republic of China on a diplomatic level that political motivations were decisive. The same was true, though unadmitted, of the American recognition of the Soviet government in 1933.

The United States is not alone in this behavior. Most other states share the same motivations in their recognition policies. Their political-opportunistic behavior can be disguised so easily as respectable objectivity because the concepts and facts of state and government are not precise. The criteria the international society has established for states and governments are quite subjective, although claimed to be reasonably objective. Some of them are: the state must be civilized; must be self-governing; must be peace-loving; must be able and willing to fulfill international obligations; must be stable and enduring; must have been legally established; must be law-abiding. Either the definitions or their fulfillment of these criteria depend very much upon the judgment of states. Each state has discretion in determining whether any or all of these criteria are fulfilled.

The political nature of recognition is further evidenced by the possibility of recognition by degrees and successive stages, for instance, de facto, de jure, provisional. Sheer practicality may be responsible for these gradations. States may have to deal physically with a state or a government without wanting to enter into full diplomatic relations. But partial recognition also gives the recognizing state more and longer political bargaining power. As the conditions states make for recognition and as historical evidence demonstrate, recognition is an instrument of politics, clothed in legal terminology.

The political character of recognition makes the many squabbles over its legal nature a fairly futile enterprise. Whether, for instance, recognition is a voluntary act or whether a state has the right to be recognized becomes irrelevant. The same is true of the question whether recognition is constitutive, i.e., whether a state or a government come into legal existence as a result of recognition, or whether it is declarative, i.e., whether recognition merely acknowledges a previously existing situation. Other legal problems dissolve themselves readily as well (except possibly for the interests of some private individuals involved in the situation) once the problems are admitted as being political. Into this category belong the legal difficulties created by divided states or by secession of parts of existing states and by merger of states, by refugee governments and by insurgents setting themselves up in another state as the legitimate government. Any recognizing state has much leeway in deciding when, what, whom, and how to recognize. By this decision, the benefits of recognition can be rather carefully endowed on the recognized state or government.

The real importance of the act of recognition lies in these benefits for either the state recognizing or the state or government recognized. A recognized state or government can sue in the courts of the recognizing state. (But lately courts incline toward permitting unrecognized governments to pursue their rights in courts as corporate entities.) A newly recognized government can take over the assets of the old government. Recognition may mean prestige and status for the recognized and the right to acquire materiel, a consequence which may be equally important for political reasons for the recognizing state. Recognition of belligerence or insurgency of a party is equally a political act, carrying with it political benefits for both sides.

The entire legal regulation of recognition—whatever is to be recognized—is an elaborate circumvention of formal legal rules states created for themselves in the first place, and which in any case do not make much sense. The possibility that several states withhold recognition from a given state or grant it to different degrees and in different stages simultaneously certainly is not helpful to the social order of the international society. The law, whatever its precise meaning, does not even have here the saving grace of attempting to regularize the use of political discretion and power. It is the handmaiden of both and its dependency upon politics becomes brutally evident.

The principle of recognition could, of course, be used for other objects. There is no need, inherently, to limit it to states or governments. But so far, the principle has been used in the main to keep states as the major actors and governments their representatives in the international society.

How much longer states can maintain their preeminent position will depend upon the volume and contents of international relations. As the division of labor across the globe proceeds, as interaction grows and turns into interdependence, as "politics" is challenged by "economics," the greater will be the pressure of those having common business or interests across national borders upon the monopolistic position of states. In the past more than today groups engaged in international transactions—from missionaries to investors—have found the support of the state in their enterprises beneficial. But they are also experiencing, increasingly so, the interference of their state in their business as a detour and, at worst, a nuisance. The possibility of creating or themselves becoming new subjects of international law is an attractive proposition for many. Reasons of state as extraneous considerations to their transaction could be eliminated and a new pluralism across national borders could have a beneficial effect upon peace and social order. But exactly these possible consequences lead states to oppose the creation of new subjects of international law and in doing so they have the massive support of their citizenry. For when the question of the state's survival arises and the power potential to guarantee it, the answer everywhere still remains that everything must be done to guarantee both, and that includes leaving states in control of international law.

NOTES

1. The Pope declared in February 1929 (Acta Apostolica Sedis XXI, 1929: 105) that there was no true and real sovereignty in the world except that based on territory. Accordingly, under the Lateran Treaty with Italy in 1929 Vatican City was created as a separate territorial entity as a means and guarantee for the independence of the Holy See.

2. Cf. Friedmann (1964: 213-231), Lador-Lederer (1963: 657-678), and Mosler (1962). The International Court of Justice in the Right of Passage case (1960: 6-144) accepted the possibility that the practice of individuals in their private capacity (crossing a piece of Indian territory in commuting from one part of Goa to another while Goa was still Portuguese) can establish a practice which can turn into international public law. See also Barberis (1969).

3. There are several international instruments in which the fundamental rights and duties of states have been stated. See, for instance, the Convention on the Rights and Duties of States, signed by the American Republics in 1933 at Montevideo; the Charter of the Organization of American States, signed at Bogotá in 1948; Resolution 2131 (XX) of the United Nations General Assembly, adopted in 1965; Resolution 2625 (XXV) of the United Nations General Assembly, adopted in 1970; and the Draft Declaration on the Rights and Duties of States of the International Law Commission, prepared in 1947.

Chapter 7

INEQUALITY

Inequalities among men as individuals or in groups are a cause of frustration and hostility. Although men have searched, they have not yet found a method or a system of undoing the consequences that trouble them. Certainly not if equality is conceived of as identity: identity of rights and obligations, benefits and deprivations, conditions and situation of existence, and so forth. But even if it is conceived more correctly as proportionality in creating and sharing wealth according to capacity and need, as adequate opportunities open to everyone, or above all as the absence of all inequalities not caused by nature (see Laski, 1948: 152-165), men have nowhere yet achieved a degree of equality to satisfy a general sense of justice. To legislate equality is futile. For a situation exists here where law is insufficient to prevent politics from exploiting it in favor of the more powerful.

In the international society this weakness of the law is aggravated by two factors. The first is that equalities between states are rarer and inequalities more extreme than between citizens. The second is that the lack of a powerful central authority making citizens relatively more equal in political power and, hence, less able to exploit their inequalities (at least in democratic systems) permits all potential dire consequences of inequality to become actual.

With the alternative of a central government excluded and many states eager to maintain or improve their position in the hierarchy of states, the one principle they have agreed on is to recognize each other's sovereign equality—as the United Nations Charter calls it. They do not know exactly what that means. But it seems to satisfy their collective egos. More important perhaps, and unexpected by the inventors of the concept, it developed into a useful instrument for disadvantaged states to press for more substantive, material equality.

Until about the end of World War II, there was a rank order among states based on international comity and striving for improved political status. But within the established hierarchy, states were fairly quiescent about their place. The Norwegian prime minister J. Hambro, shortly after the war, appealed to many newer states to reconcile themselves to their particular status, as most of the smaller states of the old world had done. Consensus prevailed that equality among states was applicable mainly to the legal sphere. The discrepancy between formal legal equality and factual material inequality was more or less accepted as a fact of life. It caused restlessness and unhappiness, but no concerted effort on the part of the low status states to use legal equality as a means of obtaining more substantive equality. To make that attempt was an innovation by the states of the Third World, eagerly supported by the Communist states.

"Equality Before the Law"

The interpretation of equality among states as equality before the law has a long history and far-reaching agreement.[1] In the treaties of Westphalia (1648) the legal equality of states was stipulated. In the French Convention, Abbé Grégoire advocated a Declaration of the Rights of Nations paralleling the Declaration of the Rights of Man in which states would be required to treat each other as equals. For centuries states have claimed that the equality of states is one form of international justice. But disagreement developed rapidly when it became necessary to define that equality— though it did so more in theory than in practice. For among statesmen it was important politically, mainly to win friends and to influence people, to pretend that everybody was equal to everybody else. Léon Blum of France once told the Assembly of the League of Nations (1936: 28) that "There is not, and we trust there never will be, an order of precedence among Powers forming the international community. Were a hierarchy of States to be established within the League of Nations, or were a governing order to be set up outside it, then the League would be ruined, both morally and materially, for it would have overthrown the principle on which it was founded." But the problem of the discrepancy between legal equality and factual inequality could not be talked away. The existing "order of precedence" is exactly the problem and the only way of solving it was to interpret legal equality in a manner not too blatantly in conflict with reality.

International lawyers inside and outside international conferences had several proposals for the formal reconciliation of substantive inequality among states with their equality before the law. One was that since states were composed of men equal by nature, states were equal by nature. A variation on this theme was that equality was an inherent attribute of independent states. A third proposal was that agreement among states that they are all equal made them equal. A fourth and probably most widely accepted proposal was that equality may mean either equal capacity for rights or equal protection of whatever rights a state had. A fifth proposal was that equality, together with independence, was an essential prerequisite or resultant of a society.

The unsatisfactory nature of all these proposals led, once again, to a demand for separating the realm of law from that of politics—which was, in fact, merely adding some more proposals. In legal situations, it was said, the assumption of equality was proper and feasible; while in political situations the reality of inequality must be accepted as a fact. In arguing this position, lawyers made reference to the equality of citizens before the law but not in political reality. Another more disingenuous argument has been that treating states as legally equal was essential to allow them to be in fact unequal as a consequence of their sovereign independence. Finally, the formal, if not cynical, argument has been made that legal equality exists as a principle, but that weak states have been unable to benefit from it, while powerful states have been able to violate it.

In the practice of states, the idea of equality among states gave rise to a plethora of generalities with little guidance as to their meaning. The United Nations Charter's "sovereign equality" is singularly unhelpful. So is the appendix (1949) to a United Nations Assembly resolution (375 [IV]) that "every State has the right to equality in law with every other State," or Article 6 of the Charter of the Organization of American States stipulating that "States are juridically equal, enjoy equal rights and equal capacity to exercise these rights, and have equal duties. The rights of each State depend not upon its power to ensure the exercise thereof, but upon the mere fact of its existence as a person under international law."

Lawyers more than practitioners tend to defend the notion of the OAS Charter that legal equality comprises equal legal capacity. Yet this is no more than a wishful assertion that states possess equality of rights and functions. International courts are inclined to accept the other version of legal equality, namely, that states are equally protected in the rights they possess and are committed to equal fulfillment of their obligations.[2] They hold this view in the full and often regretful awareness that there may be great differences between equality in law and in fact, and they do so by referring to the principle of equality rather than by interpreting it. Their reluctance to commit themselves to any precise meaning may be due to the fact that nobody doubts the validity of the principle of legal equality, but that its content changes with the needs and spirit of the times.

It changes, in particular, with the role power is playing at any given moment in the development of the international system, which, in turn, depends largely upon the changing instruments of power. For the social problem of reconciling legal with factual equality is, first and foremost, as E. H. Carr has pointed out (1949: 166), that "The constant intrusion, or potential intrusion, of power renders almost meaningless any conception of equality between members of the international community." States will not forego taking advantage of their power for their benefit. The two principles of sovereign freedom and sovereign equality enable them to do so: the first allowing states to use their power according to their discretion, the second to do so for their own benefit without outside restraint. Smaller, weaker states are not any more willing than large powerful ones to abandon these principles. For occasionally it provides them with a measure of protection and even some political influence, for instance, when votes become relevant. Much of the time, however, the principle of legal equality is little more than a fig leaf to cover naked power play between states. Equality before the law means little when the law itself results from an unequal distribution of power and therefore tends to confirm rather than ameliorate inequalities. Nevertheless, the smaller states are convinced that their salvation lies in a firm legal system guaranteeing justice based on the equality of rights, for only then, claimed an official from Madagascar (United Nations, 1974h: 106), could true meaning be given to the maxim that between the strong and the weak, it is freedom which oppresses and law which protects. But since there exists no such legal system, the principle of legal equality continues to be psychologically frustrating to many states because it in fact contributes to the denial of the very justice which is allegedly the reason for its being in the first place. The Third World states are right in emphasizing that formal equality before the law without substantive equality is not justice. That all men are created equal needs social implementation to assure that they do not become unequal after creation. The need is for not penalizing men and states for natural inequalities, and for eliminating the inequalities produced by men. To reach this goal by legal means alone is clearly impossible, but the states of the Third World are trying to use them as one of the vehicles bringing them nearer to it.

Legal Equality and Factual Inequality

The recent efforts to bring legal and material equality into greater concordance are often made in the name of democracy. But as pointed out earlier, democracy in this instance is misuse of the concept. Anthropomorphizing states results in losing the individual, when the whole essence of democracy is rescuing and preserving him. Moreover, equality in the mere mathematical sense of one equals one and a majority carries over the minority has long since been proved to be only one aspect of equality. To forbid the prince and the beggar equally to steal bread is equality with justice (and democratic) only if the law also evens out inequalities in economic, social, political, and other matters to obviate the beggar's need for stealing. The "have" states have consistently opposed any such measures. And, indeed, their past attempts to deal with the problem of inequality have usually ended in confirming it, undemocratically, whatever the external appearance of the various methods has been.

The freedom of the seas, Open Door policies, most-favored-nation clauses, and a "place in the sun," although allegedly designed to give all states equal opportunities, have in fact always benefitted those capable of exploiting these opportunities. Measures for neutralizing inequalities have had similar practical results: balances of power, alliances, regional organizations, common markets, free trade areas, and collective security systems. Then there was the practice, of recent vintage and increasing popularity, aiming at something resembling "distributive justice" in reverse—because the practice tended to favor those already in privileged positions over other states. Examples are weighted voting, proportional support and contributions, or proportional benefits, related to international organizations. These arrangements turned into benefits of the privileged states through the criteria applied. These had to do with wealth and ability to pay; use and degree of participation; interest in the organization's purposes; or the presumed power of the state (Anand, 1970; Gardner, 1965; de Russett, 1954, 1955). The more a state fulfilled these criteria, the more it benefitted. Finally, there were attempts to make inequalities invisible by transferring their political consequences into the "smoke-filled rooms" of international meetings. There either a select circle of the more important states set the stage, and thereby largely controlled, what was to take place in public meetings, or some pressuring, arm-twisting, and wheeling and dealing occurred away from public knowledge. The formal legal equality was maintained. Every state had one vote. But in fact such votes were often merely legitimizing the preceding exercise of superior power taking place behind closed doors. It was to be expected that many of the Third World states would find intolerable a situation in which the rich are getting richer and the poor poorer.

These newer states have no monopoly on the demands for substantive equality. Hitler proclaimed that all peoples ought to have an equal share in the world's goods (Carr, 1949: 165). More recently, a similar conviction was expressed by other governments.

The Dutch delegate to a meeting dealing with international law (United Nations, 1964f: 7) said that "it was not possible to express equality in terms of the sovereignty of each State. It would be more appropriate . . . to recall that equality was before all else a principle which should guide the international community in its effort to 'promote social progress and better standards of living in larger freedom' and to 'employ international machinery for the promotion of the economic and social advancement of all peoples'." A French delegate amplified this statement by remarking (United Nations, 1964a: 5) that "Unfortunately it was in the nature of things that juridical equality was not always accompanied by *de facto* equality, but it was characteristic of the spirit of the age that efforts were being made by States individually and collectively, to minimize *de facto* inequalities through economic, technical, scientific and cultural co-operation." A Swiss delegate to the Third Law of the Sea Conference (United Nations, 1974g: 21) said the strict application of equality could have inequitable results; sharing must consider the needs of the most disadvantaged countries.

BALANCING LEGAL AND FACTUAL INEQUALITY

The goal of the newer states was summed up by the Group of 77. In referring to the trend toward greater discrepancies between states, they proclaimed that "The international community has an obligation to rectify these unfavorable trends and to create conditions under which all nations can enjoy economic and social well-being . . ." (United Nations, 1967b: 5). This claim has become the leitmotif of all their statements at all international occasions. They want to use international legal commitments to eliminate substantive inequalities. Their affirmative action program is to compensate for the consequences of past inequalities and to neutralize future inequalities. China with her century-long expertise in unequal treaties provides leadership and moral support. By practically identifying legal with factual inequality (Hsiung, 1972: 82-85), it encourages other states to define legal equality as equal legal capacity. They therefore applauded a motion introduced by Yugoslavia at a meeting dealing with international law (United Nations, 1964b: 149) which included in the definition of sovereign equality "the right to legal equality and to full and equal participation in the life of the community of nations and in the creation and modification of rules of international law" as well as the entitlement of states "to every assistance on the part of the international community in making such equality effective, particularly in the economic field." Similar applause greeted the statement by the delegate from the United Arab Republic that "the economically advanced countries were under the obligation to do what they could to narrow the gap between themselves and the underdeveloped countries" (United Nations, 1964a: 9).

The tactic of these states is to exploit the well-established principle of legal equality for results normally obtainable by frankly political means. But these states do not own strong political means. They are too poor to drive hard bargains. They are too weak to enforce material equality. So they are using propaganda, appeals to conscience—especially the bad conscience of ex-colonialists—and the high repute of the principle of equality to produce legal commitments decreasing the effects of inequality.

Moreover, instead of walking the arduous road toward new norms obliging states to share their wealth, these states are trying the route of interpreting existing norms to establish that such an obligation is already a fact. Equality is, for instance, interpreted to include all kinds of equality, especially economic equality. A Rumanian official asserted (United Nations, 1966e: 4) that "The economic aspects of the principle of sovereignty could not be separated from its political and legal aspects, for economic independence was one of the main guarantees of the effective and complete exercises of State sovereignty." Illegal coercion is interpreted as including political and economic pressure—neutralizing thereby the superior power of the major states. Sovereignty is interpreted as entitling all states to participate in multilateral conferences and international organizations, or in the solution of international problems. Public goods become the "heritage of mankind" and are to serve everybody, but "taking into special consideration the interests and needs of the developing countries."[3]

The claims and proposals by these newer states amount to an abandonment of the principle of reciprocity in international law (Schröder, 1970: 60-63; Binder, 1965: 204). The meetings of the United Nations Conference on Trade and Development, especially, are making quite clear that the concessions toward equality are one-directional: from the "have" to the "have-not" states—with very little mention of efforts, let alone legal obligations, by the underprivileged states to improve their own lot. The emphasis is, instead, upon "distributive justice," more particularly its "distributive" part, as some states frankly recognize. It is not the kind of justice or the kind of policy hitherto forming the foundation of international law.

Most older states oppose the tactics of these newer states. They concede that inequality and dependency among states are unfavorable to reciprocity and the balance of interests as guarantors of effective law. Nevertheless, the incorporation of the principles advocated by the newer states into international resolutions is not recognized as giving them binding force. A major difficulty, in their view, is that with no neutral, objective international authority in sight, there is little prospect of finding a universally acceptable key for ranking, weighting, or otherwise evaluating comparatively the conditions of states for purposes of equality. The Chinese point out that "only mutual benefit is genuine equality" and that merely formal mutuality is insufficient (Cohen and Chiu, 1974: vol. 1, 131) is subject to the same complaint. There may be some rationalizing and unwillingness to sacrifice in the argument of the older states, but it has some cogency nevertheless (see Falk, 1962: 311). Under the conditions of the international system, there is virtually no way of avoiding the political confrontations to achieve new legal norms, and political concessions will be made as a rule only if they can be justified by national self-interest. A change in the meaning of traditional legal principles is likely to be universally agreeable only if it serves the purposes of the relevant states. Yet, as the newer states can point out, the political methods used in the past to make occasional exceptions to the principle of equality (e.g., in the Security Council or the International Monetary Fund) have not been encouraging for underprivileged states. Most of the important exceptions were not made to make weaker, poorer, or smaller states "more equal." They were made to legitimize the "superior inequality" of the more powerful states. There are extremely few instances (of which perhaps the General Assembly may be one) in which more powerful states have weakened themselves or altruistically abandoned something to bring the principle of legal equality more in line with factual equality.[4] It was not surprising therefore that in the Special Committee on Principles of International Law Concerning Friendly Relations and Cooperation Among States, the formulation of the principle of sovereign equality was not innovative. To the regret of the newer and the relief of older states it was essentially repeating what had always been regarded as the formal consequences of the principle (United Nations, 1970: 792).

One reason for the failure of states to solve the problem of inequality is the insistence of all upon maintaining the present international system. Under the régime of sovereignty, the tendency is for states to meet as total entities whatever specific interests bring them together. As long as the main obligation of states was to leave each other alone, this was a reasonably feasible approach. But as the need arises for more cooperation, and the individuality of states: their resources, capabilities, facilities, and so forth begins to weigh more heavily in their external relations, the approach becomes inadequate. A better equalization among states is foreseeable as states interact on the basis of specific functions and interests rather than as indivisible, homogenized "actors."

Toward Greater Equality?

If equality is viewed from the standpoint of limited shared interests states may have and fulfill through cooperation (instead of states meeting as entities in confrontation), the principle of equality may have a better chance of realization. This perspective is customary within states. Individuals are more often treated as role players than as human beings. Legal consequences attach to their natural inequalities (babies have no vote). Man-made inequalities are often compensated for, however inadequately (poor children receive scholarships). Equality is to be achieved by giving unequal rewards to people in proportion to their inequalities (Aristotle's distributive justice). Equality is preserved and justice saved by maintaining the proportion equal and steady. But the important point here is that the inequalities of people are always treated in regard to specific purposes (while only in the abstract are all men considered created equal): higher taxes for rich taxpayers; social security payments adjusted to the size of a family;

and so forth. Only where a purpose is common to all individuals as human beings are they treated alike: everybody has the right to live, therefore everybody has the absolutely equal right to self-defense.

Similarly, as the division of labor spreads across the globe, states meet more often in specific capacities (producers of wheat, manufacturers of cars, suppliers of techniques) than as total states. In such cases, their great inequality as entities becomes less relevant; they become more equal in regard to the specific purpose which brought them together and in whose pursuit they cooperate. The politicization of their relationships will not even then be entirely excluded—the system does not allow it. And the advantageous effects will be felt the least in multipurpose, essentially "political" institutions like the General Assembly or the Security Council of the United Nations. The equalization in functions will most likely be most influential in narrow, specialized international institutions and conferences with less comprehensive and more single-purpose objectives.

For example, Argentina and Brazil participate with the major nations in some agricultural organizations because of their significance in this field. In the Universal Postal Union consensus without formal vote is preferred (and works!), or the majority principle prevails when votes become necessary, mainly because the power potential of a state has little relevance for the efficiency of the postal system. Marine resources and sailing across the oceans are similarly of concern to all nations and at least in some respects independent of a nation's power. The conferences on the Law of the Sea were therefore trying to work with consensus and equality was a prominent subject. Yet these conferences also illustrated—in addition to and apart from complications arising from power differentials—how the need for the use and exploitation of the "common heritage of mankind" may reduce inequalities, on the one hand, and how difficult, on the other hand, it is to agree on methods for reaching consensus or to define equality among totally unequal factors (e.g., island, maritime, and land-locked states).[5] Continuing difficulties notwithstanding, these examples show the tendency of overall inequalities among states treated as entities to become submerged in specific mutualities leading to more equal relationships.

This tendency will progress with the increasing division of labor and benefit the efficacy of law. But the progress is slow and in the meantime total inequalities magnify. The well-endowed states will be induced thereby to preserve rather than to abandon their "superior inequality." An appeal to high-sounding principles of equality and justice will not likely make them share their wealth. Indeed, nothing is likely to produce such magnanimity. They are likely to deal more on a basis of equality with other states when it pays them to do so. The prospect therefore is that a rapprochement between legal equality and factual inequality will more likely be achieved through step-by-step treaties of limited scope and great specificity of their purposes, carefully worked out in preceding political processes, than by flourishing international declarations unrealistically trying to legislate material inequalities out of existence or pressuring developed states into sacrificing their wealth.

NOTES

1. On legal equality in general, see Dickinson (1920) Jessup (1945), Boutros-Ghali (1960 II), Fleiner (1966), Friedman (1971), and Klein (1974).

2. Few decisions refer directly to the equality of states. Most of them deal with equality of persons under minority treaties. See, e.g., Norwegian Shipowner Claims (1922: 65-66); Reparations for Injuries case, of the International Court of Justice (1949: 177); Minority Schools in Albania case, Permanent Court of International Justice (1935: 18-22); German Settlers in Poland case, Permanent Court of International Justice, (1923).

3. This particular formulation was used in a United Nations General Assembly resolution (1968: 5-6) but can be found in a similar version in many international declarations. During the discussions of the concept sovereign equality, many states introduce habitually all kinds of grievances, claims, and ambitions in the hope of having them legally taken care of in the name of legal equality, such as the right to the exploitation of national resources; the right to remove foreign military bases from national territory; the right to participate in multilateral treaties (see, e.g., United Nations, 1966: 5-6). In virtually every case, these matters have been traditionally included as special cases of the general principle and there was no need to cite them in a general formulation of the principle (see United Nations, 1966g: 15).

4. The Soviet international lawyer G. I. Tunkin (1974: 348, 440) rationalizes the special privileges of the big powers in the Security Council as a protection of the smaller powers against the "imperialist powers," in which, of course, he does not include the Soviet Union. The principles of socialist internationalism mean, according to him, that the principles of equality and noninterference "include, for example, not only the mutual obligations not to violate each other's respective rights, but also the duty to ren-

der assistance in the enjoyment of these rights . . . ." On this ground, the Soviet intervention in Czechoslovakia in 1968 was legally justified whereas "the ballyhoo raised in the bourgeois press" about it was not.

5. For an example of the practical difficulty of applying equality, see the discussions about a Sea Authority during the Third United Nations Conference on the Law of the Sea (United Nations, 1974f: 5-44). For a discussion regarding the difficulty of methods for reaching consensus, see the discussions during the preparatory work for that Third Conference (United Nations, 1973c: 16-32) and the survey of Sohn (1975: 333-340).

Chapter 8

CULTURAL HETEROGENEITY AND INTERNATIONAL LAW

Law reflects social values. The logical prerequisite for making it acceptable to its subjects is therefore their agreement upon these values. On this point, international law has two problems. The first is that in the hierarchy of values among states, their own national, not the international, society is at the apex. The second is that value systems vary from state to state. This diversity of values or, more generally, the heterogeneity of cultures in the international society has been held responsible for the ineffectiveness or even the impossibility of international law.

The Argument Against International Law

The argument dates back to the time when international law was developed in the Western world and applied only among "Christian" and "civilized" states. The Statute of the International Court of

Author's Note: This chapter represents the essence of though is not an exact replica of my article "International Law in a Multi-Cultural World," *International Studies Quarterly,* Vol. 18, No. 4, December 1974, pp. 417-440.

Justice still refers to principles of law "recognized by civilized nations" as one source of law. The argument received a slight shift and a big boost from the ideological warfare of the 1930s, the Cold War in the 1940s and 1950s, and finally from the birth of the new states of Asia and Africa.

Effective law, the argument runs, requires consensus on values. Yet the main consensus among states is a divisive one: that every state may live in sovereign independence; and so is the one common emotion: nationalism. Abstract and rhetorical commitments to peace and the brotherhood of man are belied by people's attachment to their nation and the behavior of states. The seemingly unifying spread of modern technology is decried as a surface phenomenon, unable to overcome the world's division into national societies, functioning in their own psychic environment and devoted to their own inner order. There is lacking the common sentiments and attitudes, the common values and agreement on their hierarchy which, the argument concludes, are the necessary foundation for an effective legal order.[1]

The dispute is not purely theoretical. Governments have used the argument for expedient political purposes. It allowed them to profess high values while pursuing contrary policies. The Christian states were free to colonize the "heathens." The racist basis postulated for international law by the Nazis and later by the Fascists permitted them to commit genocide in accordance with their own legal convictions. The class character Communists ascribe to international law permits them to be selectively obedient to rules of that law. The humanitarianism of the "free world's" international law allowed the victors to hang war criminals in Nürnberg and Tokyo without circumventing their law. To each his own international law!

The newer and non-Western states understandably dislike this discriminatory approach to international law. Judge Ammoun in the North Sea Continental Shelf case (1969: 134) insisted that these distinctions were neither ethical nor legal and, besides, responsible for the aloofness of many new states from the International Court. An official from Togo, with strong support from officials of other newer states stated flatly (United Nations, 1960c: 157) that "the age of 'savage tribes' had gone." Nevertheless, international lawyers remain concerned that cultural differences affect the possibility and efficacy of international law. They seek to overcome cultural barriers—as they see them—to the progress of international law by developing common denominators from different cultures (à la Julian Huxley's [1947: 7] "scientific humanism" for UNESCO) upon which universal rules of law could be based. The surprising aspect of this effort is that it is undertaken in the face of the historical evidence over several hundred years that states accept and obey international law.[2] The assumption that cultural differences are very relevant to international law does not withstand closer examination on either empirical or analytical grounds.

THE EMPIRICAL EVIDENCE

The practice of states clearly indicates their acknowledgment of international law. They continuously enter into commitments they consider legally binding. They act in accordance with rules they recognize as having legal character. And they argue their conflicts of interest, voice their grievances, and formulate their demands in legal terminology universally used and understood. The importance of international law as a means of communication is evident wherever states meet.[3]

The newer states of Asia and Africa as well as the Communist states, not belonging to or rejecting the "Western" basis of international law, not only insist upon the need and acceptance of international law as law, but also consent to many of its general principles and specific rules. Typically, a delegate to the Asian African Legal Consultative Committee (annual, 1969: 310) stated that "any legal order which tends to reinforce the rule of law is to be encouraged and supported by the small States of Africa and Asia as this is their shield." Representatives from these countries in international conferences concerned with the development and codification of international law have never advanced revolutionary demands or proposals.

On the contrary, in justifying their legal or political positions, the newer states of Asia and Africa refer to traditional principles and rules of international law. India and Iraq defended their laws relating to aliens on the grounds that their applied principles accorded with "traditional views" going back to before the days of the Reformation in Europe (Asian African Legal Consultative Committee, annual, 1960: 101). The secretariat of this Committee, in developing Asian and African positions, referred constantly to Western writers, Western practice, and "accepted rules of international law and practice." The rapporteur of the Roundtable Conference on International Law Problems in Asia, held in Hong Kong in 1967, summarized the discussions (Shepherd, 1969: Introduction) by expressing surprise that "whilst the *content* of many international law rules or even the rules themselves were doubted and suspect, no delegate advocated the changing or refurbishing of current ways and means of making or unmaking both international customary or treaty law. The constitutional structure of the world community, which in some ways at present, or so it is alleged, works in favor of the smaller nations was accepted almost without question. Regionalism, at least in terms of international law and practice, did not seem to affect those rules of truly universal legality."

The attitude of the Communist states is the same. In the Cold War, the Soviets emphasized the need to defend international law (e.g., Current Digest of the Soviet Press, 1962: 8-9; cf. McWhinney, 1963; 1967; Lissitzyn, 1965). At the dawn of détente, Professor Tunkin wrote to the London *Times* of February 25, 1963, that the Soviet Union was merely advocating "new international law," not "a new international law" or a revolution in international law (cf. also Tunkin, 1974: 35-48).

Similarly, the Chinese People's Republic declared at its foundation that "equality, mutual benefit, and mutual respect for territorial sovereignty" were its basis for international relations. It claimed the Five Principles of Peaceful Coexistence as a major contribution to the development of international law (though in fact they merely confirmed its long-standing fundamental principles).

This adoption by states of the most diverse cultural and ideological backgrounds of international legal rules originating in an era long before their births is true also of their judges at the International Court (who, however, speak as individuals). Their judgments seem devoid of special cultural influences. Judge Kotaro Tanaka wrote (1971: 15-17) that "Nine years of experience on the International Court of Justice have led me to conclude that a common basis of jurisprudence and a common language exist among the judges whereby they are able to make mutual assertions, discuss, reach agreements and disagree, in spite of their different religions, racial and cultural backgrounds." This common basis, he asserted, was the universal cultural heritage of Rome. M. Z. Khan, as president of the Court, reached the same conclusion (1972: 78). Careful studies of the judgments show that judges of the most diverse cultural backgrounds can be found in shifting majorities and that the only noticeable influence upon them all was not the culture but the national interest of their countries (Günther, 1966: 139-148; Grieves, 1969: 110-112; Padelford, 1971: 320-326; Jarvad, 1969; Hensley, 1968; Suh, 1969).

The willingness of countries which are most culturally diverse to accept the jurisdiction of the International Court is further evidence of the unimportance of cultural differences. About a third of the states which have signed the Optional Clause of the Court's Statute (Article 36) are from the non-Western culture area. Over one hundred states from that area stipulated in treaties the jurisdiction of the International Court in contentious cases, and several states of that area have actually appeared in such cases before the Court as parties (International Court of Justice, annual, 1971-1972: 12-13, 55-85; Syatauw, 1969; Coplin and Rochester, 1972).

This acceptance of the Court's jurisdiction is balanced, or perhaps overbalanced, by its rejection, or at least by reservations about it. An examination of the reasons for such negative attitude indicates, however, that they are shared by states from all culture areas, including the Western, and that, in fact, cultural differences are not conspicuous among them. Rather, the coolness toward the Court is essentially founded on fear that inequality of power among states would cause either the law applied or the judicial decisions to be disadvantageous to smaller states. The Thai government, for instance, explained its "retrenchment" from the Court's jurisdiction by preferring to wait for the day when the bigger nations were "prepared to participate more on the grounds of equal footing" (Shepherd, 1969: 128). A Cuban official explained that "in an atmosphere where power prevailed over justice it could not reasonably be expected that the decisions of a body consisting of third parties would be fair and effective." His Mexican colleague felt that "the difficulty of finding a system that would be free from political pressure" was largely responsible for the refusal of smaller and newer states to use the Court (United Nations, 1969a: 261, 274).

The alternative of regional international courts has frequently been suggested as a way of quieting these fears and, more positively, of providing cultural homogeneity. With the exception of Western Europe, these suggestions have always aborted. Discussions have invariably led to the conclusion that the regional states were not ready for a regional court. They were politically divided, and, of greater interest here, they had more difficulty in relying upon their own culture-bound law than on universal general international law (see Shepherd, 1969: Introduction, 115, 117, 120, 128, 133; Foda, 1957: 162; Jessup, 1971: 106-107). The practical result is, as their treaty commitments show, a preference for solving differences among themselves by reference to the International Court of Justice—if they are willing to use judicial procedure at all.

On this last point, it has been maintained that the Communist and more often the Asian and African states prefer methods for reaching consensus rather than judicial methods for settling their disputes (Wright, 1958; Derrett, 1966-1967). The national legal practice does not bear out such preference sufficiently to distinguish these from Western states (Levi, 1974b: 431). Abundant use is made of courts in many Asian and African countries to settle contentious cases. Because of Westernization or for other reasons, significant differences in the legal systems or in international legal practice between these and Western states have been largely wiped out. Modernization requires modern laws as well. For example, as long as India flies airplanes it must have legal regulations adapted to air traffic, no matter what the ancient Hindu codes are saying. Continental European codified law finds its parallel in Hindu and Moslem codes. The lack of rigidity Africans and Asians are said to like can be found in Anglo-Saxon Common Law. And the alleged Asian and African preference for consensus can be found in the Western practice of arbitration and settlement of cases out of court. Very likely, the alleged preference for consensus rather than litigation in the international field is not so much a cultural characteristic as it is distrust of the Court in the case of the smaller states, and a hope of settling a dispute favorably through superior power in the case of the larger states.

In the face of this evidence that states of the non-Western and Communist world take the existence of international law for granted, recognize the bulk of its basic principles, and use it expediently as do all states, what is the meaning of their demands for new international law–which apparently is voiced more by older states on their behalf than by themselves (Anand, 1972: 52; Shihata, 1965: 213-214)?

The New International Law

Upon closer inspection of these demands, especially after disregarding their rhetoric, it turns out that in most cases they do not involve new law as much as new interpretations and applications of existing law. Even that demand usually appears rather modest when existing principles of universal validity are in question. Any demand for truly new law is not peculiar to these states. It can be heard everywhere because it is related to social changes and novel needs, such as the regulation of space, oceans, and the biosphere.

Earlier references here to the approaches of Communist and newer states to some aspects of international law show that in essence these states aim at a better realization of the equality of states–which is one of their ways of achieving a greater share in the world's wealth (cf. Schröder, 1970: 44; Sinha, 1965; Fatouros, 1964; Bokor-Szegö, 1970: 52-59; Anand, 1972: 62; Starushenko, 1969). "Not all the norms of the old law were anachronistic," said the Argentine delegate to the Third United Nations Conference on the Law of the Sea (United Nations, 1974i: 73). "What needed to be changed, basically, was the philosophy and the values of the legal order." On another occasion, the delegate from Ghana claimed (United Nations, 1963a: 52) that "International law must be purged of any rules authorizing the exploitation of a weaker Power by a stronger, so as to place all States on an equal footing."

The form these demands take differs. The Communist states condemn prevailing international rules as class law, or more precisely (because they recognize the basic principles of international law) they condemn the use of international law as an instrument of "imperialist" policies (but not as a political tool as such). The newer states express their demand by a condemnation of colonialism, request for amends, and insistence upon equality mainly through equal participation in international relations. They complain about the "disparity in power between some of the older nations and the new," "the imbalance between the interests of the developed and developing states," and the advantages of the "bigger and stronger powers" (Shepherd, 1969: 127, 132, 133; Asian African Legal Consultative Committee, annual, 1969: 287, 289, 302, 305). These imbalances are to be rectified by applying the principle of distributive justice and by introducing a universal obligation of states to take into special consideration the needs of the developing countries.

The criticism by these newer states of much international law is understandable. They find that the interpretation of many legal principles and some specific rules enables more developed states to satisfy material and political interests which they share with these states, regardless of cultural differences, whereas the same principles and rules do not produce these results for them—if they do not actually frustrate the satisfaction of their interests. These states point out, as was mentioned earlier, that the manner in which international law has been applied, i.e., without their contribution, legitimized colonialism, safeguarded only formal equality, and relied upon past, (old states') practice (e.g., United Nations, 1964b: 94-95; 1964g: 11-12; 1964h: 5-6; 1966d: 11; 1968: 3; 1969a: 344).

These criticisms have been voiced by smaller or weaker states everywhere, and long before the birth of the newer states. Indeed, occasionally even larger states joined in them. The response was at least formal recognition in international instruments of human rights, equality of men, anti-racism, anti-colonialism, and fair distribution of wealth, to name a few of the desirable principles, with almost simultaneous expressions of regret that these high principles had not yet become living law. But the almost universal abstract commitment to these principles is an indication of the unity on values and consensus on principles.

The frustration of these values and principles in applied law and the unsatisfactory execution of old established principles such as sovereignty, equality, territorial and political integrity, and pacta sunt servanda are rarely due to cultural differences. They are due to the politics of the international system, denying the fulfillment of these values and principles and including, sometimes foremost, the internal and external politics of the very states making the most insistent demands for "new" international law.

The Communist demand for an international law based upon true state equality, the protection of national individuality, and their recently discovered international cooperation (rather than mere coexistence) is also not so new. "Socialized" and "democratized" laws are their new names for old rules. The Five Principles of Peaceful Coexistence are old wine in new bottles. Max Huber discovered in 1910 that international law was changing from a guarantor of the state in isolated existence to a sponsor of states in solidary cooperation. The ideological conceptualization of traditional legal principles in any case is belied by the behavior of Communist states, which is no more nor less in line with that of most other states regarding international law. It was belied also by G. Tunkin, acting as a Soviet delegate to a United Nations meeting, when he branded as false the charge that the Soviet Union and the African and Asian states were "destroying the 'homogeneity' of the international society and thereby undermining the foundations of international law." Rather, he argued, the proposition that international law had to be founded upon "common ideology and cultural unity" was "entirely mistaken." These nations supported international law, he declared, as the "best means of preserving both their independence and world peace" (United Nations, 1961c: 137-138).

The Communist approach, or at least that of the Soviet Union, to these problems of international law can hardly be explained by frustrations stemming from unequal treatment and lack of power. Their contradictory attitudes, with ideological preachings denying their practice, are explainable by the political need to justify their interests and actions in ideological terms—usually ex post facto. The approach of the newer states of Asia and Africa is determined by the uneven application of principles all states accept and by the desire to satisfy, with the help of international law, primary national interests which are amazingly alike across the globe. The roots of the demand for a "new" international law can thus be found not in cultural differences among nations, but in the frustrating results of an international political system whose basic features all states, paradoxically, cherish and support (see Friedmann, 1964: 297; Stone, 1960; Wilk, 1951: 667; Rubin, 1973: 321; Chiu, 1966: 266).

The manner in which states use law in their international relations, the culturally neutral behavior of international judges, the practice of international courts, the style of judicial behavior everywhere, and the substance of the new law demanded by many states of the most diverse cultural background show remarkable similarities and few cultural idiosyncrasies. The conclusion from the empirical evidence that the weakness of international law is hardly due to the cultural heterogeneity of the international society can be reinforced by the results of a more theoretical examination of the international society, international law, and the connection between them.

The Evidence from the Nature of Things

In analyzing the nature of law and its relation to national cultures in the international society, we must clearly distinguish between textbook law and living law. Textbook law may indeed express Christian, European, Communist, Islamic, and Hindu ideas. The writer can introduce whatever ideas he wishes and do all the philosophizing he wants to. Living law is what nations actually practice as they struggle to survive as individual entities. International politics shows only the most tenuous, if any, connections with national cultures, including ideologies—with the exception of universal nationalism. Political alignments, voting patterns, conflicts and cooperation, and economic and cultural transactions in international relations have no consistent correlation with cultural similarities or dissimilarities. But there is a direct correlation between politics, power, wealth, and the degree of a state's participation in international relations as well as the substance of these relations. A nation's culture and—contrary to popular belief—prevailing ideology are fairly independent of its international relations (Rummel, 1975; 1972: 108; Sullivan, 1972: 135; Levi, 1974a: 46-56; and the summaries in Jones and Singer, 1972: 273-395).

The overpowering wish of all states—Christian, Jewish, Hindu, Moslem, Communist, or whatever—is to exist in sovereign independence, and it permeates and politicizes all international behavior (Levi, 1974a: 28-31, 196-198). It leads to inescapable behavioral consequences and informs the substance of international law, leaving little room for cultural idiosyncrasies. Nationalism as the sentimental foundation and power as the most salient operating factor of the international system are sufficiently comprehensive to provide an identical mold for all international behavior. This is the behavior law is called upon to regulate to which a nation's culture is fairly extrinsic. The international system enforces a like interpretation of the basic features of national interests everywhere. The behavior to translate these interests into policies and actions is confined rather narrowly within the needs of social existence; the requirements of the international system; the interweaving interests of some 150 states; and the preference for regularity over irregularity in social life.

Revolutionary behavior in the international system is rare. Acceptance of the main precepts of international law, many of its rules, and individual treaties is routine, even to the point where the international behavior shows little resemblance to the internal practice of states. Parliamentary practice in international conferences is followed by states never applying it at home; legal formalities are practiced internationally which are despised in internal affairs; cases are argued internationally in legal terms by states rejecting them in their own courts; and legal principles are advocated internationally (e.g., human rights) most vociferously by states denying them to their own citizens.

Everyday experience eliminates the possibility that the legal terminology in these interactions among states is not understood identically by all states. International conferences dealing with legal questions show minimal misunderstandings and those dealing with international disputes evidence an accurate representation of claims and counterclaims in legal language. Disagreements seemingly over legal questions are most often disagreements over political ends to be achieved by legal rules. Frequently these are situations where the law, even when it fails to control behavior, still serves effectively as a means of communication (McDougal, 1960; Gould and Barkun, 1970: 136-149; Coplin, 1968). Law becomes indispensable exactly because it can be understood regardless of cultural differences. It enables states to formulate their differences and their agreements of interests in fairly clear, precise, and universal language. Law effectively bridges rather than emphasizes cultural differences.

This possibility highlights an important aspect of the relationship between a nation's culture and the role of international law. States do not normally enter into relations as total entities. Their legal or cultural systems are not necessarily mutually relevant to each other. Interactions between states are on specific issues (except in war). Any one of these issues could be devoid of a particular cultural coloration and be culturally neutral. States establish contact for some specific purpose: an exchange of goods, the reception of tourists, the stabilization of currency, a need for landing places. They agree or disagree on the conditions for these purposes without any reference to the cultural basis of these purposes. Compromises and adjustments to achieve agreement on these matters and to guarantee the requisite behavior are not equivalent to compromises and adjustments of a state's entire culture or even of an essential part of it. The interests states develop and the international methods they use to satisfy them are very much alike, unfortunately not often in common. Conflicts do not originate often from cultural differences. They arise from like but mutually exclusive interests. The weakness of international law stems less from different outlooks and much more from similar but clashing interests antagonistically pursued. In a conflict situation what counts for the contestants is not the other party's cultural system but the result of a cost-benefit calculation regarding alternative actions (Henkin, 1965 I: 191-200). In the international society more than in any other reciprocity appears to affect the balance sheet most decisively (Hassner, 1964: 53-56).

The existence and efficacy of international law depend little upon a nation's culture and vary much with the complementarity, mutuality, interdependence, disharmony, or exclusiveness of the interests states pursue. The fate of international law is determined by the relationship between specific interests held by different states, at different times and by the most promising way of satisfying them. National cultures need not be a hindrance when states wish to agree on the regulation of their interests and behaviors on the international scene. The Soviet international lawyer Evgeni Korovin had to agree (quoted in Erickson, 1972: 11) that the incompatibility of socialist and capitalist law notwithstanding "each of them, carrying out its own line and directed by its own motives, might be interested in supporting and preserving a certain amount of generally binding legal norms in international relations." Similarly and inevitably in the face of the facts, the Chinese had to come to the same conclusion, pointing out that socialist and capitalist international lawyers can be bedfellows, although they may dream different dreams.

Beyond the specific interests bringing states into contact and requiring legal regulation is the more basic necessity for law making coexistence possible. Where there is a society, there is law. There are inherent elements in a social situation independent of the society's culture. When groups wish to or have to live side by side, they must have rules about their mutually relevant behavior. They represent the essence of the minimally necessary law. They can be found in every legal system, for instance, that agreements must be kept or that some lives must be preserved. From that basic level on, laws can differ according to the nature of the society and its political system. This situation explains why in modern international relations some universal rules of international law and some of its general principles are virtually inevitable and devoid of specific cultural content, but also why states so often try to circumvent them. In any case, mutually complementary self-interest—especially that of coexistence—leads states to create and adhere to international law. The important thing is the creation and adherence, not the cultural origin and character of the self-interest (Wilk, 1951: 667). It is thus quite true to say that for a rule of law to exist there must be agreement on the underlying value. But it is quite another and erroneous statement to say that for international law to exist there must be agreement among national legal systems in toto.

That point may be reached in some distant future, when the volume, intensity, and interweaving of interests among states reach a level paralleling that of nations. But the point at which the world becomes one is so far in the distance that there is little need to worry about it in the present. What is happening now is that states develop ever more international interests making their requisite interaction fertile soil for the growth of international law. The process is accompanied by acculturation, and respectively, national deculturization. The adoption of similar ways of living creates uniformities in social existence across the globe, including the law that goes with them. Another by-product of this process, though much less pronounced, is the birth of an international culture among those who interact: officials, merchants, tourists, and students. These international publics, especially the officials, are forming an international élite sharing behavior and understandings, at least in their respective spheres of personal interests, whose roots are no longer in their national cultures (see Modelski, 1970; Walbeck, 1973). With the broadening of people's horizons in a "shrinking" world, parochial adherence to one's traditional way of life is becoming increasingly difficult. The acculturation process affects basic aspects of the international political system, including its legal part. The growth of international law is facilitated, of which the existing volume of law is the evidence.

The decisive character of interests as a determinant of the growth and effectiveness of international law also is responsible for the relative irrelevance of ideology in international politics generally and international law in particular. Although ideology is part of a nation's culture it is important to single it out here because a general assumption is frequently made that ideological differences prevent peaceful international relations. An examination of ideology (see Levi, 1970) will show it to be extremely flexible as a guide to action in international affairs. The values and beliefs of an ideology are always stated in general, broad terms. They are not necessarily internally consistent and some are held with greater intensity than others. In every concrete case, how an ideology is interpreted, which values and beliefs are selectively (and usually expediently) applied, and what rationalization is employed to advance one and to suppress another are determined by the interests demanding action in the first place. With "national" interests being most powerful, the role of ideology is generally reduced to serving, as Jeremy Bentham put it (quoted in Snyder and Wilson, 1949: 511), as their fig leaf. Whatever creation, application, or interpretation of international law is required to serve these interests, ideology will be used to justify, not specify, either. A striking recent example of such state practice was offered by the differing commentary of the Brezhnev Doctrine by the Soviet Union and the People's Republic of China, both allegedly dominated by Communist ideology. China, playing the role of protector of national independence, castigated the Soviet intervention in Czechoslovakia in 1968 as an illegal breach of sovereignty. The Soviet Union, determined to keep control of the Communist camp and obedient buffer states, announced a doctrine of limited sovereignty. In both cases Communist ideology was used to provide an interpretation of international law enabling each party to do what its interests demanded.

The subordinate role of ideology is symptomatic for the role of national cultures in general in international law. The systemic influences upon the behavior of states far outweigh those of national cultures. The conditions under which men have chosen to coexist in the world express fundamental interests and dictate methods for their pursuit essentially alike for all states. This common denominator has enabled the international society to create so many different international organizations and so much international law that virtually every conceivable interest is covered. Each of the international organizations represents a consensus on its purpose and on some of the means to achieve it. The sum of these purposes very nearly equals the sum of the purposes states pursue in international relations. In some instances (e.g., Antarctica, outer space) consensus was possible perhaps because the interests involved were esoteric and exotic; in other instances (e.g., biosphere, oceans) because the interests could not be monopolized by a few states. But in no instance had culture much to do with either consensus or its absence.

That in spite of much agreement on so many international purposes there is no common government or no complete, adequate international legal system is due to the lack of an overarching, highest-ranked common purpose of maintaining an orderly international society. There is no community for which cultural differences are only minimally responsible, if at all.[4] The existence of such a purpose would represent an integrating force upon the various international organizations. In its absence, these organizations with their varied purposes exist side by side, with little coordination toward a peaceful international order. This fractionated coexistence of organizations is replicated by the fractionated or "individualized" (Charles de Visscher, 1968: 139, 143, 160, 257) nature of the international legal system. It is not due to cultural differences. Ironically, it is largely due to the one interest all states have in common and to the one truly universal cultural feature of wanting to maintain their state in sovereign independence at all cost. Or perhaps it would be more correct to state that this fractioning is due to the willingness of people everywhere to translate that universal interest and cultural feature into reality. There are other values which all recognize: human rights, equality, and self-determination, for instance. But only lip service is paid to them or inconsequential international declarations are drawn up in their favor. These generally acknowledged cultural values have not produced legally binding norms. More often they have served governments as a screen behind which to deny these values to their own populations. Clearly, the inadequacy of international law can hardly be blamed upon the mutually antagonistic defense of cherished cultural values by nations. Rather, it is rooted in the pursuit of mutually antagonistic interests which the peoples of the world are unwilling to subordinate to a higher common interest of international peace and order.

NOTES

1. Bozeman (1971), Northrop (1952: 80-81, 259-295), Wright (1958; 1959), Castañeda (1961: 40), Schwarzenberger (1962: 294-296), Hassner (1964), Carlston (1962: 44-47), Corbett (1951: 117-119), and Tunkin (1974: 21-35) who surveys writings of several Western authors.

2. See Verdross (1964: 12-13), Henkin (1965 I: 216-225), Freeman (1959), Gould and Barkun (1970: 216-224), Falk (1966 II: 37-40), and the writing of Wilfred Jenks. Cf. also Schwarzenberger (1962: 65-82; 1939: 56-77).

3. Bozeman (1971: 3-14) does not agree with this position. For a critique of her position, see Rubin (1973: 319-324).

4. In the by now vast literature on integration and community there is far-reaching agreement that similarities in culture are among the least important factors bringing about and sustaining political community. Interests emerge as the most important factor. In discussing the role of culture in this general context, a distinction should be made between culture as the origin or cause of phenomena and culture as a tool of governments to influence the public in support of or against those phenomena.

Chapter 9

INTERNATIONAL LAW AND INTERNATIONAL CONFLICT

Conflicts are the moments, according to Thucydides, when human nature bares its teeth and men trample upon the law. Yet the existence of conflict is the major justification for law and at the same time the best test of its efficacy.

Conflict arises because a scarcity of goods makes the full satisfaction of most interests impossible. Social conflict exists when groups are interacting to frustrate the attempt by any one to obtain, maintain, or retain possession of some good which only one of them can have. The more intense the desire for the good the more likely will there be "disorderly" behavior, and the greater will be the strain upon the social organization to maintain order. For the management of conflict is the function of the entire social organization and of all social institutions—albeit to different degrees. The efficacy of any one institution to exert social control is dependent upon the efficacy of all others. In examining the efficacy of law as a foremost institution for the control of social conflict, it will therefore be useful to examine first the part of law in the context of other social controls.

Law and Other Social Controls

The entire organization of national societies is geared toward the maintenance of social order. Each part, whatever its main function, also contributes toward that end. The socialization of citizens, the institutions of politics, the legal system, the production of wealth, and the practice of religion are among the systemic arrangements aiming in interaction and mutual support at minimizing the number of conflicts, reducing their intensity, settling them peacefully, legitimizing some and illegitimizing others. If, for instance, people internalize the moral tenets of their religion, they are likely to be "law-abiding" citizens; if the economic system provides adequate material satisfactions, citizens will have little cause to disobey the law.

The integrating element of these subsystems of the society toward the management of conflict is the citizen's sense of community and his correlated highest loyalty toward the independent nation. Citizens are conditioned to respect the hierarchy of public interests with the nation at the apex. The relative importance, or better, unimportance, of all other interests is the foundation of the national social system. Lesser interests will not be allowed to interfere with the highest interest. The social tolerance for conflict is thereby greatly increased. Conflict can exist without escalating to the point of representing a serious threat to social order. As a general rule (because exceptions occur) conflict behavior within national societies is subject to the requirements of the social order (Levi, 1974a: 147-199).

The reference to these social controls and their hierarchical ordering alone is enough to highlight the quite different situation in the international society. That society is less comprehensively organized, with no sense of community as a powerful integrating element. States do not subordinate their individual interests to some (nonexisting) overall common interest. States measure the interests of the international society by their own national interests, a standard often unconducive to international social order. Some means for settling international conflicts are uninhibited by any higher interest in the welfare of the international society. There is no limit other than the national interest to prevent the escalation of a state's international interests and the means to satisfy them. International conflicts therefore are always a potential threat to the order and peace of the international society. Such escalation is kept in bounds within national societies—when all else fails—by the catchall device of the government's preponderant ability to maintain social order, especially to prevent violence as a means for settling disputes. The rejection of this device by the international society is reflected in its legal system.

International law permits each state to judge the nature and importance of its own interests as well as the suitability of the means to satisfy them. Its freedom of judgment is essentially restricted only by limitations the state has accepted on its own volition, for instance, in treaties. A state's choice of behavior decides to a large extent whether there will be order or disorder in the international society. Many international and systemic influences toward orderly behavior notwithstanding, far-reaching autonomy in national action assures the possibility of irregular and unpredictable behavior. The international system makes, in principle, disorderly behavior as normal as orderly behavior. States cannot have a reliable expectation that the settlement of international conflicts will be achieved without the disruption of social order or peace. States must therefore feel obliged, for their own protection, to act on the contrary expectation, to act on the assumption that international order will break down. The result is endemic tensions, not necessarily between any particular states but as a condition of national existence.

The poor coordination of the various social institutions, already underdeveloped, greatly diminishes their usefulness as social controls. The burden upon international law is thereby enormously increased, often to the breaking point. The situation is aggravated by governments openly admitting, if not making a virtue of rejecting, the law for the sake of national security or grandeur. In line with Hitler's and Dean Acheson's statements (p. 60) was the proud proclamation of an Indian delegate to the Security Council (United Nations, 1961a: 9; also 1961b: 16), in justifying India's forcible take-over of Goa, that colonial questions were a "matter of faith" with Indians. "Whatever anyone else may think, Charter or no Charter, Council or no Council, that is our basic faith which we cannot give up at any cost."

India is, of course, not alone in this attitude. The willingness (though not the ability) of states to use force in reaching their goals is mainly dependent upon the intensity and exclusivity of their interests. For this reason, the institutionalization of measures for the nonviolent settlement of international conflicts has been called the central problem of international politics and international law (see de Visscher, 1968: 295; Senghaas, 1972: 369).

Law and Force

The use of force in international relations is always a serious threat to the social order. It is not socially organized as a tool of government. Rather, its timing and results are irregular and unpredictable. It may be totally destructive of the international society. As this potentiality dawned on the international society, it made an effort to protect itself against the arbitrary and illegitimate use of force for any reason. But it was done in a schizophrenic manner. States as national units continued to refine the instruments of force. But as members of the international society they agreed on measures to prevent the use of force, concentrating on a legal approach. This conscious, legal effort in practice has not been very successful. Instead, credit for less violence in direct confrontations between major or developed nations must probably go to the latent effects of increasing interaction and interdependence, plus, of course, the nature of modern weaponry.

There never has been and there is not now a universal rule of international law making war or other uses of force illegal under all circumstances. The more or less systematic enterprise of states against the use of force began toward the end of the last century. It aimed at limiting the types of situations in which force could be used legitimately, at reducing the targets against which it could be used, and at restricting the instruments for its application. For instance, the Hague conventions of 1899 and 1907 created rules of war and limited the use of forcible reprisals for the recovery of debts. The Covenant of the League of Nations permitted war only after attempts at a peaceful settlement of conflicts had failed. A Geneva Protocol of 1925 prohibited the use of poison gas and some other instruments of force. The Geneva Red Cross conventions of 1929 and 1949 guaranteed certain protections to victims of war. These piecemeal agreements could, perhaps, "humanize" the use of force. They did not generally proscribe it.

A major step toward the prohibition of all use of force was the conclusion of the Treaty for the Renunciation of War (the Kellogg-Briand Pact) in 1928. The parties renounced recourse to war for the solution of international controversies and its use as an instrument of national policy in the relations between states. The use of force for self-defense, self-help, and reprisals was left intact. The final step was taken in the Charter of the United Nations. The threat or use of force in international relations is prohibited in general and for any reason or purpose. The signatories agreed in the Preamble to ensure "that armed force shall not be used, save in the common interest." In Article 2(4) they declared their willingness "to refrain in their international relations from the threat or use of force against the territorial integrity or political independence of any state, or in any manner inconsistent with the Purposes of the United Nations." Thus, the use of force legally is left only to the United Nations or to individual states in self-defense against an armed attack.

THE WEAKNESS OF LEGAL CONTROL ON FORCE

The wishfulness of a law prohibiting the use of force is readily demonstrated by the contrary behavior of states. The Indian official (cited earlier) admitted readily that the use of force was always regrettable "but so far as the achievement of freedom is concerned, when nothing else is available, I am afraid that it is a very debatable proposition to say that force cannot be used at all." There are many other reasons why states, including India, have used force. Ignorance of these reasons, or more specifically ignorance of the conditions under which certain reasons may lead states to use force, is, however, only one among the problems making it difficult to interdict legally the use of force.

One very obvious problem, bedevilling many other aspects of international law-making and law application, is the absence of an internationally recognized neutral agency. Because law is virtually always stated in general, abstract terms, an agency to interpret the law for the specific case, to define the facts of the specific case, and to determine how the law so interpreted and the facts so defined relate to each other is indispensable. The International Court could serve as such an agency, but states reject its services in the vast majority of conflicts. They substitute themselves and their judgments for such an international agency, with the most deleterious consequences for the effectiveness of law in eliminating the use of force.

The structure of the international society represents a fundamental problem for the effectiveness of the law (see Hoffmann, 1971: 39-47). States can legally possess the instruments of force and use them unilaterally. When they decide to do so they can be effectively constrained only by the counterforce of other states, if these choose to apply it. This counterforce too can be a unilateral measure, for instance, in the case of self-defense. The Charter of the United Nations envisaged this as the sole such case and substituted the collective security system for unilateral counteraction to a state's illegal use of force. But the system is nonexistent for practical purposes; partly because it has never been adequately implemented and partly because the assumptions on which it is based are faulty. Under these conditions, the law prohibits the use of force, but allows it under exceptional circumstances to be defined by every state itself. Such a law can at best be minimally effective.

A third problem is the very negative approach of the law to a prohibition of force. Simply forbidding force leaves out of consideration the possibly legitimate interests driving states to the use of force, "when nothing else is available" (to use the Indian's phrase). The law prohibiting force is likely to be effective only if states have other means for a reasonable satisfaction of their interests. The effectiveness of forbidding people to steal bread could be greatly enhanced by laws assuring everybody an adequate share of food. Without some correlation between the nature of the interests and the legal regulation of behavior for their satisfaction, legal behavior for the settlement of international conflicts is likely to be used only if this can satisfy the interests of the parties. For instance, the law on the treatment and protection of diplomats is usually effective because it takes adequate care of all the states' interests.

The lesson is that law must be concerned not merely with behavior to be tolerated or prohibited, but with the interests involved and—an impossible condition—the point at which states will use force to satisfy them. The International Court of Justice in the Anglo-Norwegian Fisheries case pointed out the relevance of interests when it stated that the economic interests peculiar to a region are part of the evidence for customary law. In one way or another, interests are the entire rationale of legal rules. It is altogether inevitable that law gets involved in interests when it regulates behavior, forbidding some, tolerating some, and demanding some. In view of so much ignorance about the reasons for states' behavior, the preferable route to making law effective would be to provide for the satisfaction of as many interests as possible through law in the hope that none will make it worthwhile for states to use force.

Harold Laski's formulation is appropriate here too that law will command allegiance when it strikes such a balance that emerges as satisfied is greater than can be secured on any alternative program. The more recent formulation of this idea is that states make a cost-benefit analysis before deciding whether to obey or break the law (Henkin, 1965 I; Northedge and Donelan, 1971: 109, 154). Some such assumption was underlying the vast network of contemporary international organizations. They provide a functional alternative to war by catering, with peaceful means, to almost every interest states pursue. But they do so, of course, only within the limits set by the international system, which means that states can still, though they may not, use force to reach their goals.

The difficulty of the law-maker remains to know how states conclude that it pays to be legal or illegal. Often the decision makers themselves do not know the answer. Moreover, the process leading up to the use of force, especially when this assumes the form of war, is rarely one step from nonuse to use of force. There are many steps between (as, e.g., demonstrated by the Cold War; Schwarzenberger, 1967: 41; Hoffmann, 1971: 43-44; McDougal and Feliciano, 1960: 243-246; Gould and Barkun, 1970: 192-197). A whole succession of steps can intervene, from friendly conversations, via tough bargaining, increasing pressure, threatening coercion, to violence. Such seamless escalation by all parties in an unbroken chain of action and reaction is normally too subtle to be defined in clear-cut legal concepts, let alone to be legally controlled step by step. The Charter of the United Nations therefore avoids such definition and instructs the members to seek a settlement of their conflicts by peaceful means if a dispute "is likely to endanger the maintenance of international peace and security" (Article 33 [1]).

The best chance for law prohibiting the use of force to be effective is an arrangement whereby on balance the interests of a state are better served by lawful behavior than by the use of force. Many international organizations have been structured to represent such an arrangement. The use of force in fulfillment of one interest is self-defeating when cooperation is needed in fulfillment of other interests (or when the possibility of retaliation nullifies advantages from the use of force). The more numerous and weighty the links of interests between states, the less useful becomes the use of force and the greater becomes the opportunity to bargain for the peaceful settlement of conflicts (Northedge and Donelan, 1971: 136-142). International organizations have as one of their functions to augment interweaving interests among states and to suggest their mutual adjustment for the benefit of all. To the extent that they are successful, the efficacy of law prohibiting the use of force will be increased.

Law and Nonviolent Methods for Conflict Settlement

The multiplicity of international interests and the multiplication of international relations to take care of them have had two contradictory results. One is an increase in the opportunity for conflict. The other is the need for cooperation with a diminishing chance of settling those conflicts by force.

When the bulk of customary law developed, the interests connecting states were relatively dispensable. Those interests at stake in conflicts—a piece of territory, access to a resource—involved little cooperation for their satisfaction and allowed confrontation. The use of force could settle the conflict favorably at least for one of the parties. The change in this possibility came about not through growing goodwill among men but through a growing technology revealing the vision of a better life on condition of cooperation.

Whether the interweaving interests of states have increased or decreased the use of force is almost impossible to determine. In fact, there has been no war or otherwise little application of force in the relations between developed states since 1945. These states share the bulk of increasing interaction. The possibility exists that in addition to the deterrent weapons possessed by these states a high volume of interaction allows these states to bargain or pressure each other into compromises so that any additional gain through the use of force is judged not worth the consequences.

Another historical fact is the growing volume of international law, mainly treaties, accompanying the growth of volume in international relations. Many of these treaties, especially the multilateral treaties, were intended to be helpful, directly or indirectly, in settling international conflicts without recourse to force. They were expected to provide, in effect, a functional equivalent to war in many different ways.

One way was to develop shared interests and then to stimulate cooperation for their fulfillment. Most international organizations are devoted to this goal, serving as symbols of an international system in which states are socialized toward peaceful coexistence. These organizations respond to existing as well as anticipated interests by helping in their articulation and fulfillment through pacific and legal cooperation. They are based on the assumption that a pacific settlement of conflicts can be more easily and cheaply achieved through bargaining in their incipient stages than later when an escalated conflict becomes enmeshed in broader issues and symbolic of national passions. Peace is to be made attractive for selfish national reasons. At best, these organizations are a step toward the integration of states into an international society eventually characterized by the rule of law.

Another way of substituting for war was the building of institutions having, so to speak, the opposite effect of these organizations. They are designed to demonstrate mainly through deterrent effect the high cost of illegal violence. The lesson that crime does not pay is to be taught by marshalling irresistible force against a state using its own force illegally. The law-breaking state is to be convinced that it cannot reach its goal by illegal means. Collective security, an international police force, disarmament of all states, and the mobilization of "world" public opinion are the suggested methods. Their initiation as a result of majority or unanimous international decisions is presumably giving them more legitimacy and effectiveness than the imposition of sanctions against a lawbreaker by individual states.

A third way of obviating war is the use of institutions for the peaceful settlement of conflict, most of them involving a third party. All these institutions are well regulated by law, but not applicable on the basis of general rules of international law. They become applicable as a result of express agreement by the parties to the conflict, a cause of some debate among states. The issue was whether the choice of these methods was up to the parties or whether certain ones had to be used under given conditions. The issue arose because negotiation—one of the methods—was, on the one hand, indispensable, if the parties had a choice of the method to be used, but on the other hand, was also considered potentially disadvantageous to a small, weak state in conflict with a big, strong state. A Japanese international lawyer pointed out that negotiations could drag on forever if the parties were about equally strong (on this issue, see United Nations, 1966a: 4-5, 10; 1966b: 4). The Permanent Court of International Justice in the case of Certain German Interests in Polish Upper Silesia (Jurisdiction) (1925: 14) decided that in the absence of a treaty agreement, a state did not have to exhaust the negotiation process before using the other methods for the peaceful settlement of disputes. This opinion was confirmed more broadly by the General Assembly's Declaration on the Principles of International Law Concerning Friendly Relations and Cooperation Among States (1970) that international disputes shall be settled with "peaceful means of their choice."

These means are—in addition to negotiation—good offices, mediation, inquiry, conciliation, arbitration, and adjudication. They are considered comprehensive enough to cover all points on which states may be in conflict: refusal to meet; disagreement on the facts, on the meaning of the facts, on the applicability of rules, on the meaning of the rules. All these methods, except negotiation, involve the assistance of a third party: a state, an international organization, individuals. The role of such a third party can be to bring the parties together and to consent to pronouncing judgment in the case. Theoretically, the third party is disinterested and objective, wishing only to be helpful. In practice, conflicting states do not admit third parties can have these qualities. They have relatively little use for these methods; the less use they have, the less the third party's influence is on the settlement and the more serious the conflict.

The infrequent employment of these peaceful methods, other than negotiation, is not too surprising when it is recalled why in national societies parties to a conflict willingly submit to the decisions of third parties. First, normally a third party is more reliably disinterested. In an interacting world, cases will be few and far between that in some way do not affect all other states, directly or indirectly, or whose outcome in some way will not affect the political position of the parties involved beyond the direct and immediate consequences. Second, the grounds for any kind of settlement are more acceptable in national societies because the society has agreed upon them beforehand in most instances. In the international society, the unequal distribution of power and its decisive effect upon the nature of social institutions as well as upon the underdevelopment of international law make all parties suspicious about any settlement by an outsider. Third, obedience to a settlement can usually be expected within states but not so in the international society. Finally, nonsettlement of a conflict within national societies does not necessarily have catastrophic consequences for either party. Between states, nonsettlement by peaceful means may be followed by a disastrous settlement through the arbitrament of a power contest.

These three ways of banning force from international relations and settling conflicts peacefully may be summarized as increasing opportunities for bargaining and integration, organizing social coercion, and third party intercession. The first of these approaches has probably been more successful than the others. But none has yet succeeded in reliably replacing violent with peaceful methods or in assuring the predominance of law over political measures. The traditional structure of the international society continues to weaken all these attempts because people continue to cherish their state's sovereign independence. All three ways are affected by the extreme politicization of the international society and because they are functionally interdependent, the failure of any one of them endangers the success of the others.

The practice of states is continuing that they judge the importance of their interests themselves and that they will seek to satisfy them with means chosen more for their expected effectiveness than for their legality. It would be quixotic to expect that states would ignore the power factor and submit to extraneous decisions at the moment when conflict threatens their interests. The increasing choice by states of the legal way to satisfy their interests is presumably due to its also being the least costly way under modern conditions. This is a choice based not on high principle but on expediency, entailing all the uncertainties coming from such a foundation. Nevertheless, this behavior holds out the prospect that lawful behavior in international relations may prevail.

Chapter 10

THE USES AND LIMITS OF INTERNATIONAL LAW

No blanket judgment can be made about the usefulness or effectiveness of international law. Neither its extreme detractors nor defenders are either completely right or completely wrong. International law performs a number of roles and exists in various contexts. Its efficacy varies with the particular part it is given in a particular situation. Law can be a norm or a means of communication. It can appear in a harmless situation of postal relations between states or of their fighting a war against each other. A list of achievements and failures can be drawn up (see e.g., Moore, 1972: 21-40; Fried, 1971: 174-176), but its basis must be very generalized. Even in comparable situations, neither the achievements nor the failures necessarily repeat themselves. And it is usually not possible to determine whether any given result was due to the law itself or to the context in which it applied. An evaluation must remain tentative. One major conclusion can be well substantiated. There is much international law routinely obeyed by governments and applied by courts. This is the portion of the law usually ignored by its critics, or disparaged. "One does not judge international law by peaceful periods and secondary problems" argued Raymond Aron (1966: 733). There also is much international law of a controversial nature, either when stated as a principle or when applied in practice. This is the portion responsible for putting its imprint upon international law and for its essential weakness. Not unjustly so, because it is this portion serving primarily as a tool of international politics and participating in its drama. Whether the norms located within this portion are used, not used, or misused by states is largely decided by their national interests in the given case.

The Expedient Use of International Law

The character of law as a political tool is evidenced in several state practices. Before there is law, there is a political context determining what the law is to be. Even in the relatively rarer cases nowadays when law is made by judges and administrators in the course of their "nonlegislative" activities, it is safe to assume that they reflect or are responsive to political situations. When an existing law's application to a dispute is found undesirable, the dispute is termed "political," declared to be nonjusticiable, and settled by political means. Even in admittedly "legal" disputes states have circumvented or emasculated the law, perhaps in the name of "national honor or vital interests," when they considered the stakes sufficiently high not to want to risk legal defeat. And they rarely permit a third party, like the International Court, to decide legal disputes. They prefer, almost literally, to take the law into their own hands.

This approach to international law can only mean that it is used to support national political purposes, in particular to legitimize political positions on international issues. International relations abound with instances of an expedient use of law à la the mote in the other person's eye. When international law is used in such a manner, the question arises whether the purpose is to settle a dispute peacefully and orderly, or whether the purpose is to embarrass the opponent, to sharpen the conflict, and to prepare an excuse and legitimization for its escalation.

It follows that a state's recourse to international law is not necessarily evidence that the state is law-abiding and cherishing international order. But there are political situations much of the time when a state's interests suggest obedience to legal rules. In such cases, the expectation of a state about the other state's behavior is fulfilled and the international society's stability is improved. On the same assumption, law clarifies the values of the international society. States know what interests and goals may legitimately be pursued; where the boundaries of their respective spheres of interest run, where they conflict, and where they overlap. Law can then assist in (negatively) preventing the growth of interests leading to strife and in (positively) creating situations for cooperation and adjustment. In either case, law can supply the parties with order-preserving methods for the settlement of conflicts and point to ways for constructive agreements. In brief, law can provide rules for all games, including the game of saving face when states in conflict wish to withdraw from the brink of disaster to the safety of legal disputation. This contingency is a compliment to international law. It shows public appreciation of legal behavior, even though states may engage in it for utilitarian reasons. This mixture of moral motivation and practical utility is in general one of the reasons for the hesitation of states to break the law openly and directly. They prefer to do so circumlocutionally, or not to commit themselves in the first place. Their opportunities for either route are plentiful.

The generality, vagueness, and interpretability of international law enable states to pretend adherence to the law while yet doing whatever their interests dictate. The justification of any political decision in some legal terms is not very difficult. Contradictory actions can usually be given a respectable legal foundation; and this can be done without any malicious intent on the part of the actions' protagonists. The ambiguity of the law, combined with the slighting of an agency able to determine with finality its meaning, enables states to escape authoritative judgment of their behavior. Even if the International Court is occasionally called upon to render a judgment, as it pointed out in the case Concerning the Northern Cameroons (1963: 37), "the use which the successful party makes of the judgment is a matter which lies on the political and not on the judicial plane." This condition is a major contributing factor to the weakness of international law, making it unable reliably to safeguard social order or to achieve justice and equality.

Ignoring the Law

Some weaknesses of international law may be located within the law itself, for instance, its lack of precision, its incompleteness, or the difficulty of finding it. Some of the work of international codification committees is devoted to solving these essentially legal-technical problems within the framework of the existing legal systems. Most of the weaknesses are rooted, however, in the international societal system (on this distinction, see Schwarzenberger, 1967: 380).

Law cannot direct, control, or enforce a behavior that states do not want to be directed, controlled, or enforced. They deliberately limit the range of law. Recognizing the need for law is only slowly inducing states to accept more regulations of their behavior. They will commit themselves to rules if they are judged to serve national welfare, not that of the international society. The two are still not effectively considered identical, although states are finding it increasingly difficult to separate the two (as their lip service to such identity shows). Hence their agreement to laws assuming the social entity of the international society with the simultaneous provision for escaping from them (e.g., the prohibition of force).

This dilemma in which states find themselves has produced the idea of the living law and the related idea of the "policy-oriented" law. Both ideas aim at bringing the law more into accord with prevailing behavior. The difficulty is to determine how close the law should be to policy or how permissive the law should be. Coincidence between rule and behavior, absence of restraint, makes law most "realistic" and obtains perfect obedience. But, as Richard Falk pointed out (1964a: 230), it also makes law "trivial."

There is no way of establishing with any precision the favorable distance between actual and legally required behavior. If the law is to have a function, it can neither be completely subservient to behavior, approving it, nor be too far removed from reality, lest it become a dead letter. Stanley Hoffmann (1971: 35) has insisted that law can be functional and effective only if the divorce between actual behavior and normative correction attempted by law is not of "scandalous" proportions. Whatever the problem of defining that proportion, some prescriptions of international law are so clearly scandalously far removed from actual behavior of states that their ineffectiveness can, in part at least, be explained by this distance.

Reducing this distance by adapting the law or the behavior is an enterprise for which the international society is poorly equipped. It can handle the problem of peaceful social change even less adequately than can national societies. The use of force is all too often the preferred short-cut method–perhaps not surprisingly so if it is remembered that within many member states of the international society this same method is applied. Even short of force, the opportunity of successfully using untamed, unregulated power makes international law many times the servant of power. It is effective mainly when there is a balance of power, a balance of interests, or both. Unwillingness among states to let power create its own harness is a fundamental cause why states can disregard the law.

This relationship between power and law becomes quite evident in the making of foreign policy. While the role law is allowed to play is obscure, the circumstantial evidence indicates that it is small. Consultation of legal officers of the government occurred with regularity in only a few countries, usually after an issue had become controversial. The addition of legal officers as regular members of a foreign office staff is a relatively recent phenomenon and has yet to take place in many countries (Strang, 1955: 159; Tilley and Gaselee, 1933: 15-118; Simpson, 1967: 9-10, 238; also Moore, 1972: 21). Typically, they act in an advisory, not in a policy-making, function. References to law are virtually absent in papers of statesmen responsible for the shaping of foreign policy, whether they be official correspondence with diplomats abroad, intra-office notes and messages, or personal writings in diaries and memoirs. International law usually occurs as an afterthought, when for a number of reasons the formulation of a policy decision in legal language appears desirable before its public appearance.[1] Among these reasons may be a need to be precise, the use of law as a tactical device, its use as a defense of the policy, or the wish to derail a relationship from a track toward confrontation to legalistic squabbles instead. Even in these cases law has its uses. But it is a use in justification, not initiation, of a foreign policy. And it may be a purely formal use, telling little about the law's effectiveness. However, the addition of legal officers to foreign offices may be the harbinger of changes related to a growing role of law in international politics.

This precedence of politics over law in matters of foreign policy can be found also in the inclination of domestic courts even of countries having an independent judiciary to accept the guidance of the executive in deciding cases touching on foreign policy questions. There are various ways in which this practice occurs, and there are differing reasons for it. The end result is always that the judiciary accepts the word of the executive as conclusive on such questions. An example of one way would be the acceptance by a court of the executive view whether a foreign government has been recognized or whether a state of war exists. An example of another way is that a court might not question the validity of an act of state by a foreign government in its own territory, especially not when questioning it would interfere with the aims of the country's foreign policy. The outcome is always the deference of legal to political considerations.[2]

Toward a Greater Use of International Law

The importance of international law appears to be growing mainly because of two factors, both reducible to developing technology: one is the changing form—but not the basic role—of power; the other, the changing volume and content of international relations. These very noticeable transformations are taking place largely independent of and sometimes contrary to national wills. The possibly favorable effects for a greater adequacy of international law may therefore take place in spite of the desires of states.

Some elements of power, unfavorably affecting the efficacy of law in the past, have lost much essentiality. The nature of extreme weapons neutralizes their use. Territorial aggrandizement, bases, and physical control of resources have lost sufficient relevance to make violent, arbitrary strife for them unprofitable. The resulting greater physical safety of states has enhanced international law relating to territory and intervention (subversion, e.g., at least does not eliminate formal sovereignty or change frontiers; and dozens of new states benefit from legal rules of sovereignty). Economic elements are effectively competing with traditional elements of power related to force. They too can be means of domination (although more so in undeveloped or unstable than in other states). To the extent that they are being so used, they are merely changing the content but not the principle of the power process. Nevertheless, however they are used, these new elements are more conducive to, indeed need more, regulation than the older traditional elements whose acquisition and use often were antagonistic to legal regulation altogether. Sometimes the laws needed to make the economic elements of power effective may be "unequal," "imperialistic," and no compliment to justice, as many weaker or newer states are wont to pointing out. Yet the relative physical safety of modern states encourages legal arrangements even between strong and weak, developed and underdeveloped states. It has demonstrably done so between developed states. There also is justifiable hope that the mentality behind economics, as an important element of power compared to that behind militarism, is favorable to the growth of international law. One reason is that with the rise of economics to greater importance in the power potential, there emerge interest groups with influence upon the making of foreign policy quite accustomed and conditioned to legal ways of doing things.[3]

The enormous growth of international law in the last few decades indicates that these conclusions are based on discernible trends, not utopian dreams (see Falk, 1964b: 14-19). The state remains the essential actor in international politics and law. But this anthropomorphication, although useful and almost necessary, should not create the illusion that any one state remains an identical entity. Changes within the state bring forth changes in its behavior. The state as an actor today is no longer the same as the state as an actor in the nineteenth century. It is today more amenable to law than it was then, partly because internally the groups influencing its behavior have changed, partly not because it wants to be but because it needs to be, partly because its conditions of existence have changed (see Goldmann, 1971: 11).

Reinforcing this trend is the other factor: the changing volume and content of international relations (quite apart from any power factor). As a result of ever-growing interests of states, they need each other for the satisfaction of these interests. Relations are established requiring legal regulations. Although interaction or interdependence may be used as a tool of power, they still need legal regulation. The effectiveness of law tends to parallel the existence of shared interests. The multiplication of such interests enhances the chance for reciprocity and this, in turn, supplies a good foundation for law and helps in creating a sense of justice. Moreover, it breaks down, to some extent, the dichotomy between large and small states—unless some small states have nothing to offer at all. Much of the law growing out of these developments remains on a bilateral or narrow multilateral basis, mostly in treaties. It best fits the small but growing number of states with fairly highly specialized relationships. In such circumstances the need for universal rules of law is limited. Such adaptability suits the dynamics of a modern international society. It contains the risk, however, of fractionating the legal system and lowering the prospect of a predictable, uniform behavior pattern by all states. This risk grows as mutual sensitivity among states to the behavior of each increases. Generally valid, universal rules for all states might then better safeguard the social order. This is one of the arguments of the newer states in favor of their right to participate in all those treaties creating either general rules for the entire society or conditions affecting the entire society. Although it has not been formally accepted by the older states, the fact is that there are more multilateral treaties with a greater number of signatories than ever before. Moreover, although the success of the International Law Commission of the United Nations and other codification agencies should not be exaggerated, they have helped, as a delegate from Iraq remarked (United Nations, 1974a: 72), in stating existing rules and proposing new rules because they "drew on all opinions expressed by States and all the practices they followed."

The Possible Future of International Law

The condition of international law in the contemporary international society is merely one aspect of its broader social context. The international society is not yet, and not likely to be in the foreseeable future, a community, in spite of the rising number of functions tying states. The emotions of people across the globe remain devoted to the state, or possibly to units smaller, but certainly not larger, than the state. However, the intertwining of relations worldwide makes behavior based on sovereign independence and splendid isolation of states extremely costly. There already is a rational awareness of the connection between material welfare and international action. Furthermore, the willingness to pay the price of reduced standards of living for the emotional satisfactions from nationalism seems to be vanishing—at least to the point where nationalism is given a content that does not interfere with voluminous international relations for mutual benefit. International law is bound to be one of the beneficiaries. People are willing to support law and to make it efficient if doing so assists the satisfaction of their interests. This last requirement must be fulfilled by political action. Law is not an instrument for satisfying interests. A formal legal order cannot create the millenium; it cannot even, by itself, create justice. Only politics can achieve that. The quality of politics and what it achieves, in turn, depend upon the attitudes of people and the interests they develop. What these are is evident in national and the international societies. Social welfare, or material well-being, is the goal dominating all politics. Under modern conditions, the inevitable effect will be the transformation of the international society from a supremely political into a mixed political-economic society (Landheer, 1964: 1-13). The metamorphosis is slow, but first results are already visible. As it accelerates the difference for international relations will be that instead of states confronting each other as political monoliths, they will meet in a more differentiated manner as producers and buyers of specific goods. Politics, in irresistibly responding to this development, will become more a promoter of reciprocal functional relations than the expression of a dominant-subject relation between states. The delegate from Cameroon to the Legal Committee of the General Assembly (United Nations, 1963d: 53) drew attention to the strength of facts when he stated approvingly "that the traditional concepts of international law appeared to have progressed under the influence of the events that had transformed international society." The state of the world provides no ground for undue optimism. But looking at international law as it was some decades ago and as it is today permits the expectation that mankind will manage to survive, which it can do only with the help of law.

NOTES

1. Compare the case studies from American practice of Scheinman and Wilkinson (1968), Henkin (1968), and Chayes (1974). For practice elsewhere, see Merillat (1964), Fitzmaurice (1965, 1968), Partsch (1970), and Bilder (1962).

2. The literature on this topic is very large. In the United States the topic is usually dealt with under the heading of the Act of State Doctrine. See Bishop (1971: 892) and Steiner and Vagts (1976: 727-728). In other countries it is dealt with under the heading of Monist and Dualist theories of international law; of public policy or *ordre public;* or generally of the role of domestic courts in international law.

3. It may be taken as symptomatic of change that the British East India Company had its own troops. Multinational, let alone the much more numerous national, corporations in international business function quite differently, more favorable to international law—even if some of them also use force and other undesirable means subversively in some countries. It would be obviously erroneous to identify all international business, or all international economic relations, with cloak and dagger methods.

Decisions and Advisory Opinions of the Permanent Court of International Justice and of the International Court of Justice, as well as other cases handled by courts or arbitrators, will be found under "Cases." Those handled by the Permanent Court are cited by year and number (as given by the Court). Those handled by the International Court will be found in the annual reports published by the Court. All documents and other publications by the United Nations will be found under "United Nations." The year in the citation of the documents refers to the year in which the statement was made (not to the year in which the document was published). ADIRC stands for Académie de Droit International, Recueil des Cours, The Hague.

CASES

Ambatielos, 1952.
Anglo-Norwegian Fisheries, *see* Fisheries.

Certain German Interests in Polish Upper Silesia, 1925, ser. A No. 6.
The Créole, 1885, 4 Moore International Arbitrations, pp. 4349-4378.
Customs Régime between Germany and Austria, 1931, ser. A-B No. 41.

Effect of Awards of Compensation Made by the United Nations Arbitration Tribunal, 1954.

Fisheries Case (United Kingdom v. Norway), 1951.
Free Zones of Upper Savoy and the District of Gex, 1932, ser. A-B No. 46.
——— 1930, ser. A No. 24.

German Settlers in Poland, 1923, ser. B No. 6.

Interpretation of the Peace Treaties with Bulgaria, Hungary and Rumania, 1950.

Jurisdiction of the Courts of Danzig, 1928, ser. B No. 15.

Kronprins Gustaf Adolf, 1932, American Journal of International Law 26 (October): 882.

Minority Schools in Albania, 1935, ser. A-B No. 64.

North American Dredging Co. (United States v. Mexico), 1970, Opinions of Commissioners, 21, 1927 (General Claims Commission, 1926).
North Sea Continental Shelf, 1969.
Northern Cameroons, 1963.
Norwegian Shipowner Claims, Permanent Court of Arbitration, 1922, in J. B. Scott (ed.) The Hague Court Reports, second series. New York: Oxford University Press, 1932.

Pacific, 1932, American Journal of International Law 26, 4 (October): 882.
Prometheus, 1906, 2 Hongkong Law Reports, 207.

Reparations for Injuries Suffered in the Service of the United Nations, 1949.
Reservations to the Convention on Genocide, 1951.
Right of Passage over Indian Territory, 1960.

South-West Africa Cases, 1966.

Territorial Jurisdiction of the International Commission of the River Oder, 1929, ser. A No. 23.

Wimbledon, 1923, ser. A No. 1.

REFERENCES

Academy of the Sciences of the U.S.S.R., Institute of State and Law (n.d.) International Law. Moscow: Foreign Languages Publishing House.
ACHESON, D. G. (1963) "Remarks on Cuban quarantine." Proceedings of the American Society of International Law, fifty-seventh meeting. Washington, D.C.
Acta Apostolica Sedis XXI (1929) in H. Heller, Staatslehre. Leiden: A. W. Sijthoff. (published in 1934)
AGO, R. (1939 II) "Le délit international." ADIRC 68: 419-554.
ALEXY, H. (1961) "Die Inanspruchnahme des IGH durch die Organe der Vereinten Nationen." Zeitschrift für Offentliches und Ausländisches Recht und Völkerrecht. (Stuttgart) 2 (July): 473-510.
ANAND, R. P. (1972) New States and International Law. Delhi: Vikas.
--- (1970) "Sovereign equality of States in the United Nations." Eastern Journal of International Law (Madras) 2 (April): 34-50.
--- (1969) Studies in Adjudication. Delhi: Vikas.
ARANGIO-RUIZ, G. (1972 III) "The normative role of the General Assembly of the United Nations and the Declaration of Principles of Friendly Relations." ADIRC 137: 418-742.
ARNOLD, T. W. (1962) The Symbols of Government. New York: Harcourt, Brace & World.
ARON, R. (1966) Peace and War: A Theory of International Relations. Garden City, N.Y.: Doubleday.
Asian African Legal Consultative Committee (annual) Report of the Sessions. New Delhi: Secretariat of the Committee.

BARBERIS, J. A. (1969) "L'activité de personnes privées et la formation de la coutume internationale d'après la Cour de la Haye." Revue de Droit International, de Sciences Diplomatiques et Politiques (Geneva) 47 (October-December): 283-288.

BENTLEY, A. (1935) The Process of Government. Bloomington, Ind.: Principia Press.

BILDER, R. B. (1962) "The office of legal adviser: the State Department and foreign affairs." American Journal of International Law 56 (July): 633-684.

BINDER, L. (1965) "The new states in world affairs," pp. 195-214 in R. A. Goodwin (ed.) Beyond the Cold War. Chicago: Rand McNally.

BISHOP, W. W., Jr. (1971) International Law Cases and Materials. Boston: Little, Brown.

BLOOMFIELD, L. (1958) "Law, politics and international disputes." International Conciliation 516: 257-316.

BLUM, L. (1936) League of Nations. Official Journal, Special Supplement No. 151, Assembly, Plenary Meetings, Part II, 1 July.

BOKOR-SZEGO, H. (1970) New States and International Law. Budapest: Akadémiai Kiadó.

BOUTROS-GHALI, B. (1960 II) "Le principe d'égalité des états et les organisations internationales." ADIRC 100: 9-73.

BOZEMAN, A. (1971) The Future of Law in a Multicultural World. Princeton, N.J.: Princeton University Press.

BRIERLY, J. L. *see* H. Waldock.

BROWN-JOHN, C. L. (1975) Multilateral Sanctions in International Law: A Comparative Analysis. New York: Praeger.

BRUNSCHVICG, L. [ed.] (1904) Oeuvres de Blaise Pascal. Vol. 13, Pensées. Vol. 2, No. 298. Paris: Librairie Hachette.

CARDOZO, B. (1934) in New Jersey v. Delaware, 291 U.S. 361, 383.

CARLSTON, K. S. (1962) Law and Organization in World Society. Urbana: University of Illinois Press.

CARR, E. H. (1949) The Twenty Year's Crisis 1919-1939. London: Macmillan.

CASTANEDA, J. (1970 I) "Valeurs juridiques des résolutions des Nations Unies." ADIRC 129: 204-331.

--- (1961) "The underdeveloped nations and the development of international law." International Organization 15 (Winter): 38-48.

CAVAGLIERI, A. (1929 I) "Règles générales du droit de la paix." ADIRC 26: 315-585.

CHAYES, A. (1974) The Cuban Missile Crisis. New York: Oxford University Press.

CHIU, H. (1966) "Communist China's attitude toward international law." American Journal of International Law 60 (April): 245-267.

CLAUDE, I. L., Jr. (1962) Power and International Relations. New York: Random House.

COHEN, J. A. and H. CHIU (1974) People's China and International Law. 2 vols. Princeton: Princeton University Press.

COHEN, M. R. (1931) Reason and Nature. New York: Harcourt Brace.

COPLIN, W. D. (1968) "The World Court in the international bargaining process," pp. 317-331 in R. W. Gregg and M. Barkun (eds.) The United Nations System and its Functions. Princeton: Van Nostrand.

--- (1966) The Functions of International Law. Chicago: Rand McNally.

--- and J. M. ROCHESTER (1972) "The Permanent Court of International Justice, the International Court of Justice and the United Nations: a comparative empirical survey." American Political Science Review 66 (June): 529-550.

CORBETT, P. E. (1951) Law and Society in the Relations of States. New York: Harcourt Brace.

COX, R. W. and H. K. JACOBSON (1973) The Anatomy of Influence: Decision Making in International Organization. New Haven, Conn.: Yale University Press.

Current Digest of the Soviet Press (1962) 13 (No. 49, January 3).

D'AMATO, A. A. (1971) The Concept of Custom in International Law. Ithaca, N.Y.: Cornell University Press.

DARJAR, K.H.R. (1960-1961) "The rule of law and economic inequalities among nations." Indian Journal of International Law (New Delhi) 1 (October-January): 276-291.

DAVIS, G. B. (1908) The Elements of International Law. New York: Harper & Brothers.

DEGAN, V. D. (1970) L'équité et le droit international. The Hague: Martinus Nijhoff.

DERRETT, J. D. (1966-1967) "Hinduism and international law, a review of K.R.R. Sastry's lectures at the Hague," pp. 328-347 in Indian Yearbook of International Affairs 15-16.

DETTER, I. (1965) Law Making by International Organizations. Stockholm: P. A. Norstedt.

DICKINSON, E. A. (1920) The Equality of States in International Law. Cambridge, Mass.: Harvard University Press.

DILLARD, H. C. (1957 I) "Some aspects of law and diplomacy." ADIRC 91: 445-552.

EHRLICH, E. (1936) Fundamental Principles of the Sociology of Law. Vol. 5. Cambridge, Mass.: Harvard University Press.

ERICKSON, R. J. (1972) International Law and the Revolutionary State. Dobbs Ferry, N.Y.: Oceana.

FALK, R. A. (1966 I) "The new states and international legal order." ADIRC 118: 7-103.

--- (1965) "World law and human conflict," pp. 227-249 in E. B. McNeil (ed.) The Nature of Human Conflict. Englewood Cliffs, N.J.: Prentice-Hall.

--- (1964a) "Janus tormented: the international law of internal war," pp. 185-248 in J. N. Rosenau (ed.) International Aspects of Civil Strife. Princeton, N.J.: Princeton University Press.

--- (1964b) The Role of Domestic Courts in the International Legal Order. Syracuse, N.Y.: Syracuse University Press.

--- (1962) "Revolutionary nations and the quality of the international legal order," pp. 310-331 in M. A. Kaplan (ed.) The Revolution in World Politics. New York: John Wiley.

FATOUROS, A. A. (1964) "International law and the Third World." Virginia Law Review 50 (June): 783-823.

FITZMAURICE, G. (1968) "Legal advisers and international organizations." American Journal of International Law 62 (January): 114-127.

--- (1965) "Legal advisers and foreign affairs." American Journal of International Law 59 (January): 72-86.

FLEINER, T. (1966) Kleinstaaten in den Staatenverbindungen des zwanzigsten Jahrhunderts. Zürich: Polygraphischer Verlag.

FODA, E. (1957) The Projected Arab Court of Justice. The Hague: Martinus Nijhoff.

FREEMAN, H. A. (1959) "Hindu jurisprudence," pp. 196-214 in Indian Yearbook of International Affairs 8.

FRIED, H. E. (1971) "International law–neither orphan nor harlot, neither jailer nor never-never land," pp. 124-176 in K. W. Deutsch and S. Hoffmann (eds.) The Relevance of International Law. Garden City, N.Y.: Doubleday.

FRIEDMAN, J. R. (1971) "The confrontation of equality and equalitarianism: institution-building through international law," pp. 231-287 in K. W. Deutsch and S. Hoffmann (eds.) The Relevance of International Law. Garden City, N.Y.: Doubleday.

FRIEDMANN, W. (1972) Law in a Changing Society. New York: Columbia University Press.

--- (1964) The Changing Structure of International Law. New York: Columbia University Press.

--- , O. J. LISSITZYN, and R. C. PUGH (1969) Cases and Materials on International Law. St. Paul, Minn.: West.

GARDNER, R. N. (1965) "United Nations procedures and power realities: the international apportionment problem." Proceedings of the American Society of International Law: 232-245. Washington, D.C.

GEIGER, T. (1964) Vorstudien zu einer Soziologie des Rechts. Neuwied am Rhein: Hermann Luchterhand.

GOLDMAN, K. (1971) International Norms and War between States. Stockholm: Läromedelsförlagen.

GOODWIN, R. N. (1974) The American Condition. Garden City, N.Y.: Doubleday.

GOULD, W. H. and M. BARKUN (1970) International Law and the Social Sciences. Princeton, N.J.: Princeton University Press.

GREEN, L. C. (1970) International Law through Cases. Dobbs Ferry, N.Y.: Oceana.

GREWE, W. G. (1970) Spiel der Kräfte in der Weltpolitik. Düsseldorf: Econ.

GRIEVES, F. L. (1969) Supranationalism and International Adjudication. Urbana: University of Illinois Press.

GUNTHER, M. (1966) Sondervoten sowjetischer Richter am Internationalen Gerichtshof. Köln: Wissenschaft und Politik.

GURVITCH, G. (1953) Sociology of Law. London: Routledge & Kegan Paul.

HALIFAX, E. F. (1938) League of Nations, Monthly Summary 18 (February): 98.

HARGROVE, J. L. [ed.] (1972) Law, Institutions and the Global Environment. Dobbs Ferry, N.Y.: Oceana.

HASSNER, P. (1964) "Le système international et les nouveaux états," pp. 11-59 in J. -B. Duroselle and J. Mayriat (eds.) La communauté internationale face aux jeunes états. Paris: Armand Colin.

HENKIN, L. (1968) How Nations Behave: Law and Foreign Policy. London: Pall Mall Press.

--- (1965 I) "International law and the behavior of nations." ADIRC 114: 171-280.

HENSLEY, T. R. (1968) "National bias and the International Court of Justice." Midwest Journal of Political Science 12 (November): 568-586.

HERCZEGH, G. (1969) General Principles of Law and the International Legal Order. Budapest: Académiai Kiadó.

HIGGINS, R. (1968) "Policy considerations and the international judicial process." International and Comparative Law Quarterly 17 (January): 58-84.

HITLER, A. (1938) Mein Kampf. London: Hurst & Blackett.

HOFFMANN, S. (1971) "International law and the control of force," pp. 34-66 in K. W. Deutsch and S. Hoffmann (eds.) The Relevance of International Law. Garden City, N.Y.: Doubleday.

HSIUNG, J. C. (1972) Law and Policy in China's Foreign Relations. New York: Columbia University Press.

HUBER, M. (1932) in J. B. Scott (ed.) The Hague Court Reports, second series. New York: Oxford University Press. (published in 1932)

--- (1910) "Beiträge zur Kenntnis der soziologischen Grundlagen des Völkerrechts and der Staatengesellschaft," pp. 56-134 in Jahrbuch des öffentlichen Rechts der Gegenwart 4.

HUDSON, M. O. (1938) The World Court 1921-1938. Boston, Mass.: World Peace Foundation.

––– [ed.] (1934 I) World Court Reports. Washington, D.C.: Carnegie Endowment for International Peace.

HUXLEY, J. (1947) UNESCO: Its Purpose and its Philosophy. Washington, D.C.: American Council on Public Affairs, Public Affairs Press.

International Court of Justice (annual) Yearbook. The Hague.

JARVAD, I. M. (1968) "Power versus equality," pp. 297-314 in Proceedings of the International Peace Research Association, Second Conference. Assen (Netherlands): Van Gorcum.

JENKS, C. W. (1969) A New World of Law? London: Longmans, Green.

––– (1964) The Prospects of International Adjudication. Dobbs Ferry, N.Y.: Oceana.

JESSUP, P. (1971) The Price of International Justice. New York: Columbia University Press.

––– (1945) "The equality of states as a dogma and reality." Political Science Quarterly 60 (December): 527-531.

JONES, H. W. (1969) The Efficacy of Law. Evanston, Ill.: Northwestern University Press.

JONES, S. D. and D. J. SINGER (1972) Beyond Conjecture in International Politics. Itasca, Ill.: F. E. Peacock.

KAHNG, T. J. (1964) Law, Politics, and the Security Council. The Hague: Martinus Nijhoff.

KAMINSKI, G. (1973) Chinesische Positionen zum Völkerrecht. Berlin: Duncker und Humblot.

KAPLAN, M. A. and N. deB. KATZENBACH (1961) The Political Foundations of International Law. New York: John Wiley.

KAPTEYN, P.J.G. and P. V. van THEMAAT (1973) Introduction to the Law of the European Communities. London: Sweet & Maxwell.

KELSEN, H. (1966) *see* R. W. Tucker.

––– (1960) Das Problem der Souveränität. Aalen (Germany): Scientia.

––– (1951) The Law of the United Nations. London: Stevens.

––– (1932 IV) "Théorie générale du droit international public." ADIRC 42: 119-351.

KHAN, M. Z. (1972) "Cinquantenaire de la Cour Internationale de Justice." Revue de Droit International, de Sciences Diplomatiques et Politiques (Geneva) 50 (April-June): 69-81.

KLEIN, R. A. (1974) Sovereign Equality among States: The History of an Idea. Toronto, Canada: University of Toronto Press.

KNORR, K. (1975) The Power of Nations The Political Economy of International Relations. New York: Basic Books.

LADOR-LEDERER, J. J. (1963) "Nichtstaatliche Organisationen und die Frage der Erweiterung des Kreises der Völkerrechtssubjekte." Zeitschrift für Offentliches Recht und Völkerrecht (Stuttgart) 23 (December): 657-678.

LANDHEER, B. (1964) "Die Struktur der Weltgesellschaft und ihre rechtliche Formgebung." Archiv des Völkerrechts (Tübingen) 12 (October): 1-13.

––– (1957 I) "Contemporary sociological theories of international law." ADIRC 91: 7-103.

LASKI, H. J. (1948) A Grammar of Politics. London: George Allen & Unwin.

––– (1931) Politics. Philadelphia, Pa.: J. B. Lippincott.

LASSWELL, H. (1963) Politics: Who Gets What, When, How. Cleveland, Oh.: World Publishing.

LAUTERPACHT, H. [ed.] (annual) International Law Reports. London: Butterworth.

--- (1970) Private Law Sources and Analogies of International Law. Hamden, Conn.: Archon Books.

--- (1934) The Development of International Law by the Permanent Court of International Justice. London: Longmans, Green.

--- (1933) The Function of Law in the International Community. Oxford, Eng.: Clarendon Press.

LENG, S-C. and H. CHIU (1972) Law in Chinese Foreign Policy: Communist China and Selected Problems of International Law. Dobbs Ferry, N.Y.: Oceana.

LEVI, W. (1974a) International Politics: Foundations of the System. Minneapolis: University of Minnesota Press.

--- (1974b) "International law in a multicultural world." International Studies Quarterly 18 (December): 417-449.

--- (1970) "Ideology, interests and foreign policy." International Studies Quarterly 14 (March): 1-31.

LISSITZYN, O. J. (1965) International Law Today and Tomorrow. Dobbs Ferry, N.Y.: Oceana.

LISZT, F. von (1911) Das Völkerrecht. Berlin: O. Häring.

LUKASHUK, I. I. (1972 I) "Parties to treaties–the right of participation." ADIRC 135: 231-328.

--- (1969) "Sources of present-day international law," pp. 164-187 in G. Tunkin (ed.) Contemporary International Law. Moscow: Progress Publishers.

MANDER, L. A. (1947) Foundations of Modern World Society. Stanford, Calif.: Stanford University Press.

MARSHALL, J. (1825) The Antelope, 10 Wheaton 66.

McDOUGAL, M. S. (1960) "Some basic theoretical concepts about international law: a policy-oriented framework of inquiry." Journal of Conflict Resolution 4 (September): 337-354.

--- and F. P. FELICIANO (1960) "International coercion and world public order: the general principles of the law of war," pp. 237-334 in M. S. McDougal and Associates, Studies in World Public Order. New Haven, Conn.: Yale University Press.

McDOUGAL, M. S., H. D. LASSWELL, and J. C. MILLER (1967) The Interpretation of Agreements and World Public Order. New Haven, Conn.: Yale University Press.

McDOUGAL, M. S., H. D. LASSWELL, and W. M. REISMAN (1967) "The world constitutive process of authoritative decision." Journal of Legal Education 19, 3: 253-300, 19, 4: 403-437.

McNAIR, A. D. (1961) The Law of Treaties. Oxford, Eng.: Clarendon Press.

McWHINNEY, E. (1967) International Law and World Revolution. Leyden: A. W. Sitjhoff.

--- (1963) "Soviet and Western international law and the cold war in the era of bipolarity inter-block law in a nuclear age." Canadian Yearbook of International Law, I: 40-81.

MERILLAT, H.C.L. [ed.] (1964) Legal Advisers and Foreign Affairs. Dobbs Ferry, N.Y.: Oceana.

MILL, J. S. (1870) "Treaty obligations." Fortnightly 14: 715-720.

MODELSKI, G. (1970) "The world's foreign ministers: a political élite." Journal of Conflict Resolution 14 (June): 135-175.

MOORE, J. B. [ed.] (1931) International Adjudication, Ancient and Modern. New York: Oxford University Press.

MOORE, J. N. (1972) Law and the Indo-China War. Princeton, N.J.: Princeton University Press.

MOSLER, H. (1962) "Die Erweiterung des Kreises der Völkerrechtssubjekte." Zeitschrift für Ausländisches Offentliches Recht und Völkerrecht (Stuttgart) 22 (March): 1-48.

NEF, H. (1941) Gleichheit und Gerechtigkeit. Zürich: Polygraphischer Verlag.

NORTHEDGE, F. S. and M. D. DONELAN (1971) International Disputes: The Political Aspects. London: Europa.

NORTHROP, F.S.C. (1952) The Taming of the Nations. New York: Macmillan.

O'CONNELL, D. P. (1965) International Law. 2 vols. London: Stevens.

OPPENHEIM, L. (1912) International Law. A Treatise. London: Longmans, Green.

OSTROWER, A. (1965) Language, Law, and Diplomacy: a Study of Linguistic Diversity in Official International Relations and International Law. 2 vols. Philadelphia: University of Pennsylvania Press.

PADELFORD, N. J. (1971) "The composition of the International Court of Justice: background and practice," pp. 288-327 in K. W. Deutsch and S. Hoffmann (eds.) The Relevance of International Law. Garden City, N.Y.: Doubleday.

PALLIERI, G. B. (1969 II) "Le droit interne des organisations internationales." ADIRC 127: 1-37.

PARRY, C. (1965) The Sources and Evidences of International Law. Dobbs Ferry, N.Y.: Oceana.

PARTSCH, K. J. (1970) "Der Rechtsberater des Auswärtigen Amtes 1950-1958." Zeitschrift für Ausländisches Offentliches Recht und Völkerrecht (Stuttgart) 30 (September): 223-236.

Proceedings of the Hague Peace Conferences: Conference of 1899 (1920). New York: Carnegie Endowment for International Peace.

RADBRUCH, G. (1932) Rechtsphilosophie. Leipzig: Quelle und Meyer.

--- (1910) Einführung in die Rechtswissenschaft. Leipzig: Quelle und Meyer.

ROOT, E. (1914) 51 Congressional Record, Part 9 (May 21): 8944.

ROSENNE, S. (1973) The World Court: What It Is and How It Works. Leiden: A. W. Sijthoff.

--- (1961) The International Court of Justice: An Essay in Political and Legal Theory. Leyden: A. W. Sijthoff.

RUBIN, A. P. (1973) "International law as a cultural excrescence." American Journal of International Law 67 (April): 319-324.

RUMMEL, R. J. (1976) Field Theory Evolving. Beverly Hills, Calif.: Sage Publications.

--- (1972) "U.S. foreign relations: conflict, cooperation and attribute distance," pp. 71-113 in B. M. Russett (ed.) Peace, War and Numbers. Beverly Hills, Calif.: Sage Publications.

RUSSETT, A. de (1954, 1955) "Large and small states in international organization." International Affairs (London) 30 (October): 463-474, 31 (April 1955): 192-202.

SCELLE, G. (1949a) United Nations A/CN.4/Ser. A.

--- (1932 I) Précis de droit des gens. Paris: Recueil Sirey.

SCHACHTER, O. (1971) "Towards a theory of international obligation," pp. 9-31 in S. M. Schwebel (ed.) The Effectiveness of International Decisions. Leyden: A. W. Sitjthoff.

SCHEINMAN, L. and D. WILKINSON (1968) International Law and Political Crises. Boston, Mass.: Little, Brown.

SCHNEIDER, J. W. (1963) Treaty-Making Power of International Organizations. Geneva: Droz.

SCHRODER, D. (1970) Die Dritte Welt and das Völkerrecht. Hamburg: Forschungsstelle für Völkerrecht und ausländisches öffentliches Recht der Universität Hamburg.

SCHWARZENBERGER, G. (1967) A Manual of International Law. London: Stevens.

--- (1962) The Frontiers of International Law. London: Stevens.

--- (1939) "The rule of law and the disintegration of the international society." American Journal of International Law 33 (January): 56-77.

SCHWELB, E. (1966) "Neue Etappen der Fortentwicklung des Völkerrechts durch die Vereinten Nationen." Archiv des Völkerrechts (Tübingen) 13 (May): 1-52.

SCOTT, J. B. [ed.] (1932) The Hague Court Reports, second series. New York: Oxford University Press.

--- (1916) The Hague Court Report, first series. New York: Oxford University Press.

SEIDL-HOHENVELDERN, I. (1967) Das Recht der Internationalen Organisationen einschliesslich der Supranationalen Gemeinschaften. Köln: Karl Heymanns.

SENGHAAS, D. (1972) "Zur Analyse internationaler Politik," pp. 347-382 in G. Kress and D. Senghaas (eds.) Politikwissenschaft. Frankfurt am Main: Fischer Taschenbuch.

SHEPHERD, V. [ed.] (1969) Roundtable Conference on International Law Problems in Asia. Hongkong: Hongkong University Press.

SHIHATA, I. F. (1965) "The attitude of new states toward the International Court of Justice." International Organization 19 (Spring): 203-222.

SIMPSON, S. (1967) Anatomy of the State Department. Boston, Mass.: Houghton Mifflin.

SINHA, S. P. (1965) "Perspectives of the newly independent states on the binding quality of international law." International and Comparative Law Quarterly 14 (January): 121-131.

SNYDER, R. C. and H. W. WILSON (1949) Roots of Political Behavior. New York: American Book Co.

SOHN, L. B. (1975) "Voting procedures in United Nations conferences for the codification of international law." American Journal of International Law 69 (April): 310-353.

SØRENSEN, M. (1960 III) "Principes de droit international public." ADIRC 101: 5-254.

STARUSHENKO, G. B. (1969) "Abolition of colonialism and international law," pp. 77-96 in G. Tunkin (ed.) Contemporary International Law. Moscow: Progress Publishers.

STEINER, H. J. and D. F. VAGTS (1976) Transnational Legal Problems. Mineola, N.Y.: Foundation Press.

STONE, J. (1974) Of Law and Nations. Buffalo, N.Y.: William S. Hein.

--- (1960) "A common law for mankind?" International Studies (New Delhi) 1 (April): 430-431.

--- (1959) Legal Controls of International Conflict. New York: Rinehart.

STORY, J. (1822) U.S. v. The Schooner La Jeune Eugénie. U.S. Circuit Court, 2 Mason's Reports 409.

STRANG, W. (1955) The Foreign Office. London: George Allen & Unwin.

SUH, I. R. (1969) "Voting behavior of national judges in international courts." American Journal of International Law 63 (April): 224-236.

SULLIVAN, J. D. (1972) "Cooperating to conflict: sources of informal alignments," pp. 115-138 in B. M. Russett (ed.) Peace, War and Numbers. Beverly Hills, Calif.: Sage Publications.

SYATAUW, J.J.G. (1969) Decisions of the International Court of Justice. Leyden: A. W. Sijthoff.

TAMMES, A.J.P. (1958 II) "Decisions of international organs as a source of international law." ADIRC 94: 261-364.

TANAKA, K. (1971) "The character of world law in the International Court of Justice." Japanese Annual of International Law 15: 1-22.

TEITGEN, P. -H. (1971 III) "La décision dans la communauté économique européenne." ADIRC 134: 588-689.

TILLEY, J. S. and S. GASELEE (1933) The Foreign Office. London: G. P. Putnam's.

TONNIES, F. (1935) Gemeinschaft und Gesellschaft. Leipzig: Fues (R. Reisland).

TUCKER, R. W. [ed.] (1966) Hans Kelsen Principles of International Law. New York: Holt Rinehart & Winston.

TUNKIN, G. I. (1974) Theory of International Law. Cambridge, Mass.: Harvard University Press.

--- (1963) London Times (February 25): 14.

UDOKANG, O. N. (1971) "The role of new states in international law." Archiv des Völkerrechts (Tübingen) 15 (August): 147-196.

United Nations:

(1975) A/Conf.62/WP.9.
(1974a) A/CN.4/Ser.A/vol.I.
(1974b) A/C.6/SR.1308-1393.
(1974c) A/Conf.62/vol.I.
(1974d) A/Conf.62/SR.29/vol.I.
(1974e) A/Conf.62/SR.22/vol.I.
(1974f) A/Conf.62/C.1/SR.2-SR.4/vol.II.
(1974g) A/Conf.62/C.1/SR.5.
(1974h) A/Conf.62/SR.28/vol.I.
(1974i) A/Conf.62/SR.23/vol.I.
(1973a) A/C.1/PV.1928.
(1973b) A/C.1/PV.1932.
(1973c) Preparatory Work for the Third United Nations Conference on the Law of the Sea.
(1972) A/C.6/SR.1364.
(1970) Yearbook of the United Nations
(1969a) A/Conf.39/aa/Add.1.
(1969b) A/Conf.39/11/Add.2.
(1968) A/Conf.39/11.
(1967a) TD/38,MM 77/1/20.
(1967b) The Work of the International Law Commission.
(1966a) A/AC.125/SR.27.
(1966b) A/AC.125/SR.29.
(1966c) A/6230.
(1966d) A/AC.125/SR.6.
(1966e) A/AC.125/SR.7.
(1966f) A/AC.125/SR.4.
(1966g) A/AC.125/SR.5.
(1966h) A/6309/Rev.1.
(1966i) A/CN.4/Ser.A/vol.I part II.
(1966j) A/6309/Rev.1.
(1966k) A/AC.125/SR.25.
(1966l) A/AC.125/SR.26.
(1966m) A/AC.125/L.38/Add.2.
(1966n) A/AC.105/C.2/SR.57.
(1966o) A/AC.105/C.2/SR.59.
(1966p) A/AC.105/C.2/SR.61.
(1966q) A/AC.105/SR.62.
(1966r) A/AC.125/SR.24.
(1966s) A/AC.125/L21.
(1966t) A/AC./L23.
(1966u) A/AC.125/L16.
(1966v) A/AC.125/SR.36.
(1966w) A/AC.125/SR.37.
(1966x) A/AC.125/SR.34.
(1966y) A/AC.125/SR.38.
(1966z) A/AC.125/SR.35.
(1965a) A/CN.4/Ser.A/vol.I.
(1965b) A/CN.4/Ser.A/vol.II.
(1965c) A/CN.4/175/I.
(1965d) A/CN.4/175/II.
(1964a) A/AC.119/SR.35.

United Nations (Continued):
(1964b) A/5746.
(1964c) A/AC.119/SR.33.
(1964d) A/AC.119/SR.17.
(1964e) A/AC.119/SR.23.
(1964f) A/AC.119/SR.34.
(1964g) A/AC.119/SR.22.
(1964h) A/AC.119/SR.24.
(1963a) A/C.6/SR.791.
(1963b) A/PV./1258.
(1963c) A/CN.4/Ser.A/vol.I.
(1962a) A/CN.4/144.
(1962b) A/CN.4/Ser.A/vol.I.
(1962c) A/PV.1130.
(1961a) S/PV.987.
(1961b) S/PV.988.
(1961c) A/C.6/SR.717.
(1961d) A/AC.6/SR.715.
(1960a) A/C.1/SR.1133.
(1960b) A/PV.956.
(1960c) A/C.3/SR.1012.
(1957) A/CN.4/Ser.A./vol.I.
(1956) A/CN.4/63.
(1955a) A/2911.
(1955b) Repertory of Practice of United Nations Organs, vol.I, Articles 1-22 of the Charter.
(1954) ST/PSCA/1 Repertoire of the Practice of the Security Council 1946-1951.
(1953) A/CN.4/63.
(1952) A/2211.
(1950) A/CN.4//23.
(1949) A/CN.4/Ser.A.
(1948) A/CN.4/2.
(1947a) A/CN.4/SR.37.
(1947b) A/C.6/SR.38.
(1947c) A/AC.6/SR.38.

United Nations General Assembly Resolution:
(1974) 3314 (XXIX), A/9631.
(1970) 2625 (XXV), A/8028.
(1968) 2467 C (XIII), A/7218.
(1965) 2131 (XX), A/6014.
(1962) 1803 (XVII), A/5217.
(1960a) 1515 (XV), A/4684.
(1960b) 1505 (XV), A/4684.
(1949) 375 (IV), A/1251.

United Nations Conference on International Organization [UNCIO] (1945) vol. 9. New York: United Nations Information Organizations.

VERDROSS, A. (1964) Völkerrecht. Wien: Springer.

--- (1929 V) "Règles générales du droit international de la paix." ADIRC 30: 275-517.

Vienna Convention on the Law of Treaties (1969) American Journal of International Law 63, 4 (October): 875-903.

VISSCHER, C. de (1968) Theory and Reality in Public International Law. Princeton, N.J.: Princeton University Press.

WALBECK, N. V. (1973) Global Public Political Culture. Peace Research Reviews 5 (November).

WALDOCK, H. [ed.] (1963) J. L. Brierly, The Law of Nations. New York: Oxford University Press.

--- (1962 II) "General course on public international law." ADIRC 106: 5-251.

WEBER, M. (1960) Rechtssoziologie. Neuwied: Hermann Luchterhand.

WESTLAKE, J. (1924) Traité de droit international. New York: Oxford University Press.

WILK, K. (1951) "International law and global ideological conflict: reflections on the universality of international law." American Journal of International Law 45 (October): 648-670.

WOOLSEY, T. D. (1894) Introduction to the Study of International Law. New York: Charles Scribner's Sons.

WRIGHT, Q. (1959 III) "The strengthening of international law." ADIRC 98: 5-289.

--- (1959) "Asian experience and international law." International Studies (New Delhi) (July): 71-87.

WRIGHT, Q. (1958) "The influence of the new nations of Asia and Africa upon international law." Foreign Affairs Report (New Delhi) (March).

YEMIN, E. (1969) Legislative Powers in the United Nations and Specialized Agencies. Leyden: A. W. Sijthoff.

YESELSON, A. and A. GAGLIONE (1974) A Dangerous Place. The United Nations as a Weapon in World Politics. New York: Grossman.

INDEX

ABOUT THE AUTHOR

WERNER LEVI was born in Halberstadt, Germany, 1912. After attending several universities in Europe, he came to the United States, where he received his M. A., 1943, and his Ph.D., 1944, both from the University of Minnesota. Dr. Levi, who is presently affiliated with the Department of Political Science, University of Hawaii at Manoa, has lectured at many universities in the United States and abroad, including several developing countries. In addition, he has held numerous research positions and been the recipient of prizes and awards, among these two Fulbright scholarships. His books include *Fundamentals of World Organization,* 1950; *Free India in Asia,* 1952; *Modern China's Foreign Policy,* 1953; *Australia's Outlook on Asia,* 1958; and *The Challenge of World Politics in South and Southeastern Asia,* 1968.